WHEN WE ALL GET TOGETHER

A Guide for the Intentional Host

WHEN WE ALL GET TOGETHER

A Guide for the Intentional Host

ALEXIS H. MOORE

Published by Selah Publishing Group, Bristol, TN. Printed in the United States of America.

ISBN: 978-1-58930-320-1
Library of Congress Control Number: 2020923546

Dedication

To my husband, *Marcel*, who encouraged me to lean into my passion and share it with the world. In moments when I felt like my cup was empty, you always found a way to remind me how valuable the work of bringing people together is and motivated me to continue on. Your encouragement to push my own boundaries has been formative to my ability to reach a coveted goal of mine. Thank you for, at times, being a student of my work, but always my partner in this thing called life.

To my first tribe – *my mom, my dad and my brother*. You've taught me how important it is to truly see and hear people. The examples you've instilled in me still resonate deeply and have made me who I am today. I will always admire how you value, care for and show up for the communities you've created. This is a team I will always be proud to be a part of.

And lastly, but certainly not least, I dedicate this book back to *God*. Thank you for entrusting the care of your people with me each and every time we assemble.

Contents

Dedication v

Acknowledgments ix

Foreword xi

Section One: Forsake Not the Assembling

Chapter One
The Crisis 19

Chapter Two
First Things First...Let's Get Back to Community 25

Chapter Three
Community is the Heart of the Solution 33

Section Two: Four-Step Vibe Check

Chapter Four
The Mindset Shift 43

Chapter Five
Step 1: Who is the Primary Focus? 55

Chapter Six
Step 2: What is my Purpose? 63

Chapter Seven
Step 3: How is Intimacy Fostered? 75

Chapter Eight
Step 4: Am I Fostering Inclusion? 91

Section Three: It's a Whole Vibe

Chapter Nine
Understand It 103

Chapter Ten
    Feel It 111
Chapter Eleven
    Create It 119
Chapter Twelve
    The Vibe Creator's Workbook 127

        Notes 133
        Author Information 135

Acknowledgements

The journey of taking this book from a mere idea to what you hold in your hands was truly a collaborative and herculean effort. Words cannot express the gratitude I have for Britney A. Stephenson and Darian Dozier who have helped me see this journey through!

Foreword

Perhaps you are similar to me, I hyper obsess about the accuracy and delivery of my intentions. I overanalyze my feelings and how to best convey them to others. The details matter to me, always. I desire for people to understand me. And even in all of that, I have found myself in places that I did not understand. I have watched myself disassociate from spaces where I did not belong. I have zoned out in moments where the energy was off, and I felt like I couldn't connect with the people. I have always been aware of the vibes in a room, its value and the importance to either create, add to, or separate from.

People have an innate need for a sense of connection and belonging in various spaces. We all want to be seen, heard, and understood. And even more, it is important to create vibes that support communing, communication and community. So of course, the feeling and intentions behind a hosted event, matter. It is the tangible outward demonstration that resonates with people. It actually says what you are trying to say.

Despite knowing that these things are true, I must admit hosting is not my gift. There, I said it. While I pride myself on displaying a certain level of care and consideration for my guests, the idea of hosting is terrifying. A nice idea that I would love to be great at doing. But the reality is that the preparation that is required to ensure that the desired outcome and intended impact is fulfilled. Well, that's a lot. And then to plan accordingly so that there are moments throughout the entire experience that embody the vibe. That's no easy feat. At least not for me. And quite frankly the very thought of hosting people or an event with proper execution, could send me into a full-on panic attack.

What is the cause of this? Like so many of you, I have been a victim of poor hospitality. And I believe that the uncertainty of my intentions meeting the expectations of execution is overwhelming. Maybe I don't want to feel the guilt of the gift of a moment that I failed to give, because I wasn't equipped with the tools to create what my guests needed. Then there is the possibility that I don't want to be accountable for someone else's experience. Or it could be that I know what it's like to be hosted and to be accepted in a place that felt like was prepared especially for me. I know what it feels like to receive a gift that I wasn't sure that I deserved. And while I would love to be the giver of that. How do you create that type of moment?

It is for all of those reasons and experiences, that I am not only a champion for positive vibes, but I am connoisseur of good vibes. I recognize that everyone has a unique responsibility when it comes to the vibe. It is for those reasons that I am sure, that we are not only responsible for reading the vibe, but we must be just as diligent about carrying the vibe with us and protecting the vibe. But what happens when you are responsible for creating the vibe? What does it look like when you have to host people which means that the vibe, energy, and overall experience is your task to lead? What should you consider? What do you do?

Just some of the many questions that cross my mind. And yet somehow, I have found my own way to connect with people and channel my mood into an experience that is impressionable. And as much as I won't consider myself the greatest host, I think I know how to create moments based on the things that I like. But is that enough? It's easier to get people interested and engaged into something that you enjoy yourself. Perhaps that is a recipe for an easy hosting gig. But what if you are late to the party, where a vibe already exists. How do you shift the energy in that room? Can you still be a good host at an event that isn't yours? I find myself peeping my head into a space to check out the music and the energy. I look around to read the people, the ambiance, and even the flow of conversation. Because I know that reading the room helps to you to stay clear of bad vibes and negative energy that could be detrimental to moments that need to occur.

Hosting is the pulse check. And it is all about the vibes that you want to create. It is unique to the creator that is creating the vibe. Hosting is more than entertainment, it is engagement, it is an encompassing experience that leaves an impact. It is an invitation to your guests to show up fully and to bring their entire being into a space. I wish there was a cookie cutter solution to hosting, a template that you can plug and play everyone into. You know some type of playbook for hosting that identifies the players and how to play the game.

Does it have to be a challenge to create a vibe and share it in such way that your guests experience it the way that you intended. Through her expertise and guidance, Alexis Moore so eloquently provides us with the information to see that intentional hosting that is well executed is a thing, and its possible. Moore encourages us to host in a way that creates a space for creativity and the curation of ideas that is coupled with intentionality at its core. She reminds us that hosting is the staple for minor details that your guests always notices and feels instantly. It's what the details say, "that I had you in mind and how you feel in this space is of value to me." Hosting gives us an opportunity to center who we think we are and position ourselves in the midst of vulnerability and the healing that comes from communing, communication, and community. Moore helps us to remember the "why" of hosting... and encourages us to check the vibe, create the vibe and connect to good vibes when hosting events or even being hosted.

Whether you are the one hosting or the one being hosted, Moore encourages us to understand hospitality is a gift to others. It is an act of service. This guide enlightens us on the responsibility of not only creating but seeking and supporting the moments that are true to our vibe and the members of our tribe. The passages help us to identify and stay focused on the intention of the moment during preparation because the moment is always a reflection of the intentions of the heart. The practices ensure that you are aware of connections and the creation of experiences. It is a step towards leaving your hang-ups at the door, dropping off your concerns on the porch and finding the tools that support the vision for your vibe as you walk into the threshold of hosting "your way" for your guests. Moore reminds us to remember the sprit behind hosting and provides us with foundational principles and tips to properly host. Each chapter helps us to strive toward the promise that we all intend to make to our guest… The promise that who they are in entirety is more than enough.

Moore helps us to create vibes that unmask issues, foster connections, promote engagement, support fellowship and strengthen relationship.

I believe that this book will help you be certain of the vibes you want to create and help you build your hospitality confidence with each page, as it has done for me. Let me be the one to say kudos to you. Cheers to you for discerning the existing vibes, identifying the vibes you want to feel, and the ones that you desire to create. May the people who have the opportunity to experience the "good vibes" you create through hosting, be better because of it. You have just expanded your hosting portfolio.
— LoVey Smith
Creative | Poet | Author

Section One

Forsake Not the Assembling

This is the power of gathering. It inspires us –
delightfully – to be more hopeful, more joyful,
more thoughtful – in a word more alive.
— Alice Waters

Chapter One
The Crisis

When crisis hits, we don't turn against each other, we listen to each other. We lean on each other. We are always stronger together.
— Michelle Obama

Our circles of family and friends are expanding geographically. We don't necessarily need to live in close proximity to connect anymore. Our phones and computers do the heavy lifting for us; until the Wi-Fi connection fails. For the sake of precious time, conversations have been reduced to choppy dialogue and short-form texts. If you can afford to dedicate a few extra seconds, you may even throw in an emoji or GIF to share deeper emotional insight. That's what these things are made for, right?

We pride ourselves on working tirelessly to prove how productive we can be only to experience burnout resulting from the competitive grind. We are so busy navigating the world from a preoccupied perspective. Working, texting, scrolling, thinking about the next move, or whatever else is captivating in the moment has us living with our heads down. We no longer make eye contact with others, let alone flash an endearing smile. Sitting in a room full of people, but no one saying a word to one another is increasingly normal. Not to mention the superficial level of social media interaction with hundreds or thousands of followers may seem sufficient. But are these connections truly fulfilling?

If you are like me, you approach a new year with very high expectations. Many of us craved a new beginning and were eager to welcome a new decade. Even saying *"the year 2020"* just kind of rolls off the tongue! It hits differently. Lots of exciting opportunities and fun times were on the horizon. According to Twitter, 2020 was supposed to be the year of vision and reflection.

Yet, despite our collective positivity, this year has been undeniably difficult. With respect to the passing of several iconic societal figures, the continuation of racial injustices, and the shock of a global pandemic that has taken too many lives, plus moved us into a financial recession, 2020 has been quite the battle. Members of our very own communities are aching and grieving in isolation. The vibe in our circles is heavy. Our country is in crisis. In-fact, the world is in crisis.

If we took a moment to lift our heads and mindfully look at others around us, that shift in gaze would reveal a troubling truth about society. The truth is, we've allowed superficial thrills to divert our attention from where it is most needed at the moment: each other. Even before 2020 threw a handful of complex situations our way, members of our society already felt isolated from one another. We didn't necessarily need a pandemic to recognize that people are suffering in silence. We've allowed an entire generation to struggle with connection and relational intimacy because interpersonal skills have faded, and are fading. While adhering to social distancing guidelines is intended to keep us healthy, being separated from each other for months on end will only deepen a pain point that we were already facing.

The year 2020 has exposed some deeply troubling aspects of society. After these revelations, things will not remain the same moving forward. Our future is as bright as the actions we're currently taking to refresh it are reflected back to us. As we collectively transition to a "new normal," we are being asked to show up as thoughtful, heart-centered agents of change. Now is when we seek ways to pour into each other with all the love and compassion we can access. This is the energy that will keep us whole.

Listen, don't be discouraged. I promise it's not all bad news. We still have space to make the year 2020 one for vision and reflection. We can choose to look at this year as our opportunity to pause, reflect, and envision what we really need in order to thrive moving forward. Now is the time to hit pause on all of that external noise, reflect on how our communities can be strengthened, and envision a future where all individuals feel empowered to show up for one another through deeply impactful connection.

The journey begins with understanding the lens from which you observe relationships, how you participate within them, and the overall impact that you create while in connection with others. Our community moves us beyond the self-interested isolation of private lives and connects us to one another.

Whether you're hosting, being hosted, or simply interested in better understanding the thought-work that goes into elevating the vibe within your community, my mission is to help you create meaningful interactions that invite people in. You will be encouraged to invite others to show up as their most authentic selves by letting them know that they are wanted and welcomed. That they are meant to be here.

As the hostess, your job does not have to be difficult. Are there a few more things to consider? Absolutely. But, do you have to go all out and jump through hoops to host the biggest comeback shindig of the year? No. Not at all. Actually, make things even simpler on yourself and understand that your only job is to nurture the moments when we are able to commune together. Create a space or environment to make everyone comfortable enough to be themselves. This one instruction can make anyone nervous. But, I encourage you to keep reading, and I'll help you realize that the journey to intentional hosting is not as intimidating as it seems.

The most important part for both parties, the host and the hosted, is to not only keep this renewed spirit towards socialization alive for your next gathering, but to apply it for the rest of your lives as you continue to foster fellowship with loved ones. When you look at life, gatherings and communities through the lens of graciousness and appreciation for just being able to be together, you help perpetuate this excitement for being with one another. This way, we don't fall back into the same bad habits of passing through life being surrounded by people, but making no actual connections with anyone.

Our mission is to expand the scope of bonding. We will explore this through the lens of hospitality and intentional hosting, which are both rooted in biblical teachings. If you've been to any planned gathering, you likely understand how vital the role of a host truly is. *When We All Get Together: A Guide for the Intentional Host* will prepare you to be in the driver's seat moving forward. As a host, your duties are to recognize, cultivate, and most importantly, protect the vibe. We are Vibe Creators. Our communities need us now. So let's get to work!

.

Chapter Two

First Things First…
Let's Get Back to Community

And let us consider one another, in order to stir up
love and good works, not forsaking the assembling
of ourselves together, as is the manner of some, but
exhorting one another, and so much more as you see
the Day approaching. (Hebrews 10:24-25)

There is plenty of progress to be made in regards to cultivating stronger, more intentional relationships. Just understand that this is indeed a collective pursuit. It's time for us to get back to one another.

Now, you may be asking, "Why do I even need community?" We all have our own reasons for how we relate to others, and circumstances can change that over time. But we were not designed to walk through life alone. Community is what gets you through the tough days and hard nights. It is what gives you a sense of belonging and unconditional safety. Our community is who we celebrate our successes and accomplishments with. Without meaningful connection to others, one can easily begin to feel lost and isolated. We aren't meant to just survive alone. From the beginning of time, we were always meant to have at least one person to lean on. For example, God gave Eve to Adam so he would not be alone (Genesis 2:18).

Social science traces community back to evolutionary necessity. Early civilizations developed systems to efficiently run a community, make sure everyone had enough food, and ensure that everyone had sufficient shelter. Unlike today, the act of gathering wasn't just something to fill a social desire, but a requirement for survival. We were intentionally and carefully designed to connect and truly *thrive together*.

You may be familiar with Psychologist Abraham Maslow's *hierarchy of needs* – an illustration and prioritization of the five basic needs for people to reach self-actualization - the full realization of one's potential. Maslow's theory indicates that one needs to matriculate through the various levels in order to achieve self-actualization. After one's basic safety needs like food, water, and shelter are met, then you arrive at our social needs on the third level of the pyramid. What are our social needs? We need friendship, intimacy, and connection with others to reach the point where we can realize our full potential as humans. According to his theory, when you are not satisfying one of these needs, then you are missing out on reaching your full potential. Realistically, it's going to be hard to maintain all five levels at the same time. However, by just having a fundamental awareness of your social needs can help you realize when you have deprived one of them longer than the others.

Cultivating a sense of belonging is easily a forgotten layer. We get busy or overwhelmed by life, and we forget to touch base or tap in with our loved ones and friends. Checking in and checking on those closest to us becomes a fleeting thought that may never actualize. How many times in your life have you committed to something, and when the time comes, you don't want to participate in it, and in our specific case, host it? But that is the beginning of what happens when we start to *forsake the assembling*. That's how easy it is to fall into the trap of unintentionally disconnecting from our tribes. It starts to happen subconsciously. We get caught up in our own chaos, that we forget others have chaos too. Everyone needs a way to decompress from and process this chaos, and that's what community is for.

Forsake not the assembling...

You'll notice that I refer to the Bible throughout this text and that's because it has been a guide for me throughout my life. Whether we share the same religious beliefs or not, there is something for everyone to gain. Each message carries its own significance, which transcends any barriers looking to further divide us. Regardless of your religion, I ask that you consider each Bible verse I share with you as a message within a framework; one that allows room for your beliefs and perspectives to be applied.

Way before I started bringing people together, I sought to develop a deep understanding of what being a host or hostess really meant. I was raised in the church and whenever I wanted to understand what was going on around me, I was encouraged to tap into my faith and search the scriptures. In my reflection of the times we are living in, I was led to read the familiar scripture Hebrews 10:24-25. Recounting the world events captured in the previous chapter, it seems as though we are going through a huge transition in our society, similar to the people in the book of Hebrews. Now, more than ever, we need revelation and understanding of the importance of assembling, and what constitutes this meaningful expression.

In the first part of Hebrews 10:25, we see "not forsaking the assembly of ourselves together, as is the manner of some." This particular part of the verse is most commonly referenced when talking about church attendance. However, I believe the message in the text extends beyond talking just about gathering "in church," because our personal ministry of loving one another goes beyond the walls of the church. In the framework of hosting, it means people should cherish gathering and engaging altogether within their communities. People gather for a number of reasons - to socialize with others, to be entertained, to celebrate various milestones, and for other various reasons. Others may gather strictly out of duty, obligation, and tradition. The "assembling together" constitutes open-participatory gatherings where we are looking for ways that we can achieve greater connection and engagement where we mutually edify each other.

An different version of the scripture says, "not giving up meeting together, as some are in the habit of doing" (NIV). As we discussed previously, people's lives get busy or the burden of hosting something is so overwhelming, that we stop making the effort altogether. Consider this -if no one else picks up the responsibility, then we run the risk that gatherings cease to continue. Before you know it, weeks or months have gone by without anyone reorganizing a meeting of people, and there goes the communal time that is so important and necessary for us all.

When you are alone, or trying to keep your own company, your thoughts can be overwhelming. You are limited to your own perspective and experiences, which are valid and valuable, but lack the benefit of diversity of thought. Incorporating diverse perspectives through sharing with our loved ones can help us get the most out of our life's experiences. How refreshing it is to share your thoughts with other people that are going in the same direction as you, but may have a different path getting there. How encouraging it is to have people surrounding you that say you can do it. Do you need a big, fancy dinner to have your closest friends encourage you towards your goals? Absolutely not. What you need is a dedicated place and time to facilitate this interaction and commit to continuing it on a regular basis. That's it. The process of hosting and connecting with friends in a fulfilling way is a lot simpler than people may think. When we think about gathering together with members of our communities or social circles and hosting an event, this is an important message to keep in mind.

The last part of the scripture illuminates our purpose in gathering, *"but exhorting one another, and so much the more as you see the Day approaching"* (Heb. 10:25). Notice the words, "consider one another" and "exhorting one another." These verses are referring to gatherings where people mutually participate in encouraging each other. Not only should we be mindful of the importance of the need to get together, but actually committing to see it through; using this time to push each other towards our purpose.

Another theory we can apply to gathering is the *social exchange theory*, which says that relationships and social behaviors occur through an exchange process. Anytime people connect with one another or look to build relationships, they weigh the *risks* and *rewards*. The things that uplift people and make them feel whole are considered rewards. Risks are represented by any exchange that makes either party feel less than.   As we intentionally cultivate relationships, the goal is to maximize rewards and minimize risks for ourselves and the people we invite in. That way, the exchange is an ongoing flow of goodness spreading far beyond the initial interaction and into other spaces as the loving energy echoes.

As you consider gathering with others, your main goal should be to tap into something positive. This can be very simple, a matter of putting together like-minded people and talking about something positive in each other's lives or in the world. What I mean by actionable gatherings are assemblies of people coming together to do something positive. Therefore, hosting doesn't always mean having to take on a multitude of people in your own home and having to make them all feel comfortable. It can be a group of volunteers going to do work in your community; something already established, you just extended the invite and show up. "Good works" (Hebrews 10:24) suggests building in a call to action.

When we assemble, we experience a joint feeling of fellow-ship with others. This is often as a result of sharing common attitudes, interests and goals. Hebrews 10:24-25 provides direction for how individuals within these groups can and should relate to one another, especially during times of un-certainty or distress. This verse, in a straightforward way, tells us what is possible, if we choose to consider one another, *love and good works*. The true power of getting together should not be taken for granted because where two or more people gath-er, there is opportunity to exchange blessings of all shapes and sizes. Whether these exchanges involve material goods, such as gifts or intangibles such as sharing emotions, every interaction is a chance to support and uplift a neighbor. This is how groups thrive.

What it comes down to is lifting each other up, learning from one another and being the friend that each other needs. Being in community gives you the chance to be around people at dif-ferent stages of life's journey and to "bear one another's burdens alongside them." (Galatians 6:2).

Are we aware of the benefits that we forgo when we live in isolation? It is for all of these reasons and benefits of why we cannot afford to forsake the assembling. When we forsake the assembly, the sense of belonging and benefits of community are lost. When we come together, we can encourage each other, share one another's burdens, celebrate, motivate, and show our love for one another. That's the goal each time when we get together. People should leave our presence better than when they came. This concept transcends any type of gathering or event because it is applicable to all types of gatherings to a certain degree.

Pause and Reflect

Throughout this journey, there will be times that I encourage to take a moment to "pause and reflect" before progressing to the next concept. I offer this suggestion to help navigate the layered approach I've taken in developing this guide. Let's take a moment to start to unpack the concept of community.

1. What was your foundational community?
2. Was there a sense of community within your family? Or did you find this elsewhere?
3. At what age did you first begin to connect with others that you felt called to?
4. How does community help you to decompress difficult feelings, situations, emotions and more?
5. During unprecedented times like these, how would gatherings be helpful to yourself and your community?

Chapter Three

Community is the Heart of the Solution

In every community, there is work to be done. In every nation, there are wounds to heal. In every heart, there is the power to do it.
— Marianne Williamson

In one way or another, what we're taught as children tends to stick around in our belief systems throughout the years. The ability to form a mutually beneficial bond with another is a primary, foundational need for all of us. Think about how an innocent, helpless newborn relies on its primary caretaker for security and nourishment. Even though this newborn is expected to grow into a self-sufficient individual who is capable of carrying their own, every single one of us still relies on someone for something. Quite literally, human connection is a tool for survival. Thus, building bonds is one of the first and most significant lessons to observe as a child because those lessons serve as examples of how one is likely to relate to others and build relationships moving forward.

In *The Art of Community*, Charles H. Vogl tells us "communities are created when at least two people begin to feel a concern for each other's welfare." From an early age, I was blessed to have learned about the value of a strong community and what becomes possible when that energy is used to uplift one another. This is not something I take for granted. My first community building experience started with a very small inner circle – the family unit. As far back as my memories reach, my mother always reminded my brother and me that we were a team. That notion still resonates with me today. When the conscious decision to act as a team is made, each member becomes more mindful of their own presence, as well as how that impacts everyone else. I becomes we; you becomes us. The capacity to have compassion and concern for someone else's well-being pushes out selfishness. At its core, a team shares a common interest and move towards the betterment of everyone involved. They celebrate each other's successes, accomplishments and happy moments. Teams also have vested interest in their team members well-being.

It is no secret that my parents were wise beyond their years. The lessons they taught my brother and me were valuable and would prove to be the foundation on which my perception of community was built. I've applied much of what they taught me and continued to develop my understanding of what belonging means to me. When I look back, I can see the thread of community running through my experiences. I've always gravitated towards roles and spaces that prioritize the art of gathering, whether I was serving as a community leader or participating as a member. So much so that, one of my biggest decisions as a teenager to attend college was based on community. I did not hesitate to attend Spelman College, an all-women, historically black college, located in Atlanta, GA.

It was a place where I naturally felt seen, understood, and un-apologetically welcomed. I was encouraged to show up and take up space as my authentic self – nothing more, nothing less. Attending Spelman taught me how to observe and honor the differences between individuals. I learned about the value of sisterhood and connecting in. I developed an appreciation for the variety of things that make each of us unique because this is where the opportunity to connect on common ground is found.

Being aware of how, when, where, and why you engage with others in any capacity, allows you to show up as a relational member of your circle. We can describe a relational being as someone who deeply acknowledges and honors the concept of interconnectedness. These are the people that can strike up a conversation with a stranger in the checkout line, somehow making them feel special within a matter of minutes! It really doesn't matter where you are or what you're doing. If your eyes are open, you'll find the opportunity to invite someone in and offer up what they need in that moment. A mindful exchange costs nothing but a little time and reminding someone that they are seen, heard, and valued is the ultimate reward.

Community is not limited to location and the people around you. In fact, we create and are a part of a variety of circles throughout life, regardless of physical proximity. Some of which we may not even realize! Within my friendship circles, I've been affectionately called "the connector." I find pleasure in cultivating spaces that draw people into one another, bringing people together from various circles who may have otherwise overlooked the opportunity to gather. We can connect people from all walks of life simply by observing what is important to them. Interactions are deepened when we take the time to focus on what's important to others and these are the moments that build genuine connection.

Allowing others to witness your compassion stands to benefit all. You may be familiar with the Butterfly Effect? Yes, the trippy, early 2000's thriller starring Ashton Kutcher! Well, the movie is based on a theory called the *butterfly effect* which suggests that a small action taken at some initial point can significantly influence a different outcome in the future. Things that seem inconsequential or completely unrelated are actually connected through an energetic flow, even if we aren't aware of it. In other words, anything you do now can largely affect the future. The theory gets its name from the work of Edward Lorenz, a mathematician and meteorologist, whose weather models anticipate the possibility of a tornado's exact time of formation and exact path to be influenced by a butterfly flapping its wings weeks before. The butterfly effect underscores the importance of investing in intentional relationships now. When we mindfully show up for one another in the present, we're presetting the table for reciprocated love in the future.

When you think about hosting, a simple way to enhance your impact is to consider what type of community you're inviting in and why. What's the deeper reason you've been brought together and how might that influence your role? Every gathering is unique. However, there are five types of communities to most can be grouped into.

Communities in Place- This form of community means you live within reach of someone unless,
you've made the decision to go off the grid and live
in complete isolation (in which case you probably
wouldn't have access to this book). Communities in
place are probably the most traditional way we think
about relating to others, as well as the broadest type.
This a collection of people who coexist within a geo-
graphical boundary, like your neighborhood or city.
You may not know everyone, and this certainly isn't
a push to knock on everyone's door to become best
friends with all your neighbors. Rather, let this serve
as a reminder that you are surrounded by multiple
sources of support from people who may care about
your wellbeing simply because you each share a similar space or environment. Communities function best
when that energy flows both ways, always.

Communities of Interest- This is a group of people
who share similar interests or passions with one another. Think about support groups for new mothers,
a book club, or even a few friends who make brunch
their mission on the weekends! Perhaps a group connects to watch the big game or attend church together.
Communities of interest are made up of people who
share enthusiasm for the same or similar passions.
This circle is a powerful tool for members to promote
skill building, hold each other accountable for growth,
and offer support for dreams and aspirations.

Communities of Action- This represents a group of
individuals who have a collective goal to bring about
some sort of change. Volunteering or participating in
advocacy groups are examples of communities that
gather for action and impact. Perhaps you or someone
you know has played a role in the social justice move-
ments of 2020. Whether one prefers to peacefully

protest throughout the nation's streets or share resources and information on social media, the same energy inspires these individuals to link together as agents of change.

Communities of Practice – Members within this assembly participate in the same profession or undertake the same activities. Your coworkers, teammates or classmates are examples of this type of group. Similar to communities in place, communities of practice often include people and aspects that are beyond an individual's control. You cannot decide who can or cannot move into your neighborhood. Nor can you always influence who your company chooses to hire or let go. Regardless, these groups still present opportunities to be of service to others and engage in mutually beneficial exchanges that uplift the collective.

Communities of Circumstance - Sometimes we are introduced to people or are bound together by particular circumstances. Without these circumstances, we may have never crossed paths with this person. I often refer to this as "divine connection." Regardless of how it happened, we should always consider why it happened and what the potential benefits are of having this coincidental meeting. For instance, this "chance meeting" could be the catalyst to help you both get through a shared circumstance. Maybe the situation introduces you to a group of people that you happened to need right at that moment. Regardless of what the future holds, think about the relationships that you have developed out of circumstances and what may flourish from that.

What's beautiful is one's freedom to engage with a wide variety of communities and thereby connect an even larger collective.

Magic happens within circles because diversity of thought and experience are present and accessible. There are many spaces that could benefit from increased representation of heart-centered people like you. Claim space for yourself and make way for another to tap in as well.

When a sense of community or a sense of belonging is established and felt, that is the start of a dynamic and rich engagement. Strong connected communities are the foundation for successful gatherings. When we have a shared interest in the purpose of the event, we tend to be better participants and contributors.

Pause and Reflect

As you can tell by now, there are many different circumstances that bring people together. Take a moment and reflect on the following questions:

1. Are you able to place yourself in a community based on each of these ideas?

2. How many different communities are you a part of?

3. In which of these communities do you feel like your most authentic self?

4. Within each of those communities, how do you show up differently?

Section Two

Four-Step Vibe Check

Once your mindset changes, everything on the
outside will change along with it.
— Steve Maraboli

Chapter Four
The Mindset Shift

Now that we have a deeper understanding of the value of and role our community plays in why we gather, let's dive right in and host our first event! Not so fast! Ok, I can hear you saying "wait, hold on! There has to be more to it." You are right. There is more ground to cover. So, hang around.

Having a firm understanding of why community is so important is not the penultimate solution to navigating the crisis mode we are in. There are more factors to being an impactful host to consider. Even I can be challenged with some aspects of hosting. I will be the first to admit, as a highly introverted person, hosting can feel draining at times. It is exhilarating in the planning, but I have to tap into a reserve of energy to be a fully present and a contributing member. It is in those moments that I am reminded of the foundation of what is needed for hosting with the best of intentions, putting the logistics to the side and considering what is important to those who are around you. This may first require a mindset shift to become aware of the very distinct difference between the various types of intentional hosting – hosting with the intent to entertain and hosting with the intent to be hospitable. This is an important concept to lock in because understanding the difference may completely change the way you engage with others moving forward.

My first experiences with intentional hosting came in the form of an opportunity to help my mother. Now, both my parents played a significant role in helping me develop my sense of awareness of how I show up in this world. However, my mother took the lead in curating the culture of our family, most notably how we steward those special moments when we engage with one another. I cherish the opportunities when she and I are able to partner together in planning events. When I was younger, I assisted her in the planning of numerous retreats. When planning a gathering like a spiritual retreat, one must be very mindful and intentional about what they are doing and why. You are inviting people into a vulnerable space. You want everyone in attendance to feel empowered and rejuvenated when they leave. The same fundamental objective is true when hosting with intentionality and mindfulness.

In addition to witnessing my mother transform lives by welcoming people in, I was exposed to other ideas and practices of mindfulness at an early age as well. What is mindfulness, exactly? By definition, it is "the quality or state of being conscious or aware of something" (Oxford Dictionaries). You may have heard this concept referenced when it comes to meditation and other forms of relaxation. But it can be incorporated into many parts of your life. My experience with mindfulness was about being aware in my interactions with others. Being mindful means moving with intention and taking action with a purpose in mind.

In addition to being considerate about how I interact with others, I also learned how to be mindful about movement within my community. When others are going through their personal challenges, what they need more than anything is to know that they have a full army behind them. So, regardless of what was going on in my community, I was taught to at least be aware of it in the first place. Secondly, I was taught to consider the larger impact of the situation and encouraged to do something about it where I saw fit. That's what being mindful looks like when hosting. It is constantly being aware of the current moment and what your goals are during the gathering. With this as our goal post, it gives us a direction to go in while planning and you build your event components around it. Every time my mother and I planned an event, a talk, or a meal, we tried to keep in mind the question "What do we want our guests to get out of this?" Guest-centered hosting starts with the end in mind. We imagine the "feels" we'd like our guests to walk away with and seek opportunities to anchor those positive vibes in moments throughout.

The host shows guests what they can expect while in each other's company and helps them align with that vibe as the gathering progresses. This made it so much easier to stay focused and not get lost in the logistics of planning. Although you may get distracted by mishaps, no shows, and the normal stresses of hosting, at the end of it all, you should return back to your goals. It's your home base. Hosting events in the context of what best serves your community reminds you why you started and makes your role that much more fulfilling. When you are hosting an event, it's also important to be aware of what you want to get out of it. Use this as your base so if things get chaotic and you find yourself questioning why you even decided to host in the first place, you have a constant reminder of what you need to do in order to create the impact you desire. Intentions keep us on course.

There are a number of hosting philosophies to subscribe to. However, there is one that resonate deeply with my hosting style – *the empathetic host*. An empathetic host knows how to "feel with" someone and is emotionally prepared to do so. This is about showing up for another with compassion while being able to put yourself in their shoes. You're essentially asking yourself, "how would I feel and what would I need to hear if I were to experience their circumstances?" Gaining a clear understanding of another's perspective positions you as a guide to what they need. By no means is this therapy. However, others who experience or witness an empathetic host in action are likely to feel a therapeutic sensation because people enjoy feeling heard and having their feelings acknowledged. Your actions as an empathetic host make that possible. Empathy is also a tool for self-reflection. It is a way of recognizing who you are by tapping into the lives of others.

I encourage you to reflect on your hosting philosophy and I want to remind you of a distinction I made earlier – hosting with the intent to entertain and hosting with the intent to be hospitable. You might be thinking "well isn't all *hosting* the same?" Not necessarily and this may deconstruct some of your preconceived notions about hosting. Good, it's supposed to. I hinted at the potential need for a mindset shift a bit earlier because I hope that realizing the key differences between these two types of hosting will remove the stress that many of us feel when welcoming others in. So much of the time we think of hosting as exclusively having something to do with entertaining others. But hosting can be a lot richer than that when we consider the impact of layering on hospitality.

Let's explore how entertainment and hospitality differ when it comes to the intent behind your hosting experience.

When you think about entertainment, what comes to mind? Does your favorite TV show or movie pop up? What about a DJ or your favorite artist? Either way, entertainment can be exciting and it serves a very specific purpose. First, entertainment is driven by the desire to put on a show of some sort – it is performative in nature. It is intended to make us happy and it gives us this momentary break from the realities of life. Entertainment is supposed to be fun. You want to leave having had a good time or you don't feel like you got your money or time's worth, right? This is what I think of when it comes to entertaining. This is also what I imagine are my guests' expectations.

As I mentioned before, when we are entertained, we can escape from life for a few moments. We don't have to dive into the depths of our feelings, fears, or reality at all. We can just be in the moment, enjoying one another's presence which is a precious occurrence. There is normally a lot of energy, happiness and laughter when we entertain others, giving them an escape from any hardships they may be facing outside of the entertainment space. We can surround each other and bask in the comfort of just having other people around. In this day and age, we could certainly use a distraction.

There is no feeling like the high after throwing a successful event. Realistically, there's a chance you may feel exhausted once everything is said and done. However, consider that there are many fringe benefits to successfully entertaining your guests - you may have even entertained someone who was inspired after attending your event. Maybe you had someone at your event such as a speaker or someone who people look up to that inspired your guests, resulting in someone feeling empowered. Not only is it enjoyable for the guests, but it also has some great outcomes for the host. Reflecting on your role throughout the process has its advantages as well. It's rewarding to receive compliments and acknowledgement of your effort, especially when you've put a considerable amount of work into something.

Entertainment certainly has its highs; but it also has some shortcomings or downfalls. At the core, it is about honoring the host, not necessarily the guests. Additionally, one of the main differences between entertainment and hospitality is that it tends to focus on things (i. e. the condition of the house, who made the guest list, food and convenience and the list goes on.) Admittedly, we all go into host or hostess mode where the focus is primarily on material things. We want the house to appear perfectly spotless, and maybe even find the outfit that will attract the most compliments! This isn't a bad thing. The desire to present the very best version of yourself to those that you welcome in is a feeling so many of us can relate to. We all want to put our best foot forward, especially if the belief is that focusing on these aspects is what shows guests that they are cared for. But contrary to popular belief, devoting all, or even the majority, of your efforts to the material aspects of an event obscures the main point of welcoming loved ones into your presence. This is the biggest distinction between entertainment and hospitality. There's a tendency to put energy into the things that are not as high-yielding. When the majority of a host's time is spent on trying to entertain others, it is easy to miss out on the true meaning of hospitality. That perspective keeps the host in the spotlight as the entertainer. Intentional hosting warrants a shift in that spotlight in order to provide an even richer experience.

To be totally transparent, it seems we've lost our way in regards to the true meaning of hospitality. We're concerned with impressing others, entertaining guests only for the sake of a good time. As hosts, the desire to throw a praiseworthy event is all too often the guiding force behind the bulk of planning and decision-making. If we look hard enough, we can see that cultural norms have shifted the way we look at hosting. The modern event is often planned according to what makes the host an interesting entertainer; but what about guests and their diverse set of needs?

Like so many other activities that we habitually engage in, the concept of hospitality, as we know it today, has grown from cultural roots planted all around the world, well before our time. This is certainly not a history lesson, but it helps to know that ancient texts spanning across a multitude of cultures have long acknowledged the vital role that hospitality plays in serving others and keeping communities meaningfully connected. Our love and need for hosting Sunday brunches, Saturday afternoon cookouts, and welcoming family into our homes during the holidays isn't all that novel. That's right. We've just updated our aesthetics, located trendier settings, and coined new sayings; perhaps all in the pursuit of presenting hashtag and Instagram-worthy events. No shame there. Can we really be sure that it happened if all of your followers can't see, "like," or comment? Debatable.

Can you recall the last time you attended an event and your first instinct was to take a "selfie?" The selfie was an opportunity to document the great time that people had in your space. But how many pictures have you willingly smiled for, but didn't feel any joy or satisfaction in your soul as you were surrounded by people? Hospitality takes that selfie and converts it to a wide-angle that puts others within focus. Instead of it being all about you and making sure that people know that you threw the greatest dinner party post pandemic, you are turning the attention towards how you can help others and how you can positively impact their lives. It is about so much more than entertaining. It's about getting to know those in your life and around your life who are yearning for human connection, love, and service. It is about God's commandment to love your neighbor as well as practicing mindfulness. The focus is on people and serving others.

You see, ancient texts show that hosting others once had less to do with entertaining setups or fascinating hosts and more to do with the sheer notion of hospitality. In religious spaces, hosting played an important role in ensuring the safety of travelers. Accordingly, opening up one's home to others became a religious practice in honor of God by overseeing the safety of his people. People were encouraged to extend hospitality to others and those who did were looked upon favorably. Long before any of us were hosting events, inviting others into personal space was deeply rooted in faith. There is an urgent calling to bring us back to the type of hospitality that provides genuine connectivity. The type that is rooted in community.

Hospitality is not so much of an act as it is an attitude of "otherness." It is about cultivating meaningful relationships. Maintaining and tending to relationship with people is referred to as stewardship. On stewardship, church planter, pastor, and author, Jeff Christopherson says:

> "Stewardship means to manage wisely and well what God has placed in our care. Hospitality is one important way that we choose to manage what God gives us. What changes might our community experience if our measure of success were the quality of service we provided to meet (and exceed) the needs of the people who enter our doors? How might we improve our hospitality to members in our family and friendship circles?"

When you view hosting through the context of stewardship, it is so much easier to hold on to how important it is and continue putting forth energy to preserve it. Let's steward people well because hospitality is a matter of stewardship. If people accept our invitation to an event, then we should be cognizant that they were divinely placed in our care. Don't let that statement overwhelm you. Let it empower you to realize the gift that has been handed to you.

After taking a moment to notice this great opportunity, really take a moment to consider how you are going to handle it. Once again, you don't have to feel overwhelmed at this thought, but simply think about how you would want to be treated if you were experiencing someone else's hospitality and wanted to feel cared for. The form that resonates with my hosting style is *subtle hospitality*. This is the kind that sneaks up on you. You may not even realize someone else is honoring you, but before you know it, you're nice and comfortable! The energy is in the small details. Little by little, people become submerged in a welcoming energy that puts them at ease. Whatever your expectations are, use that as a starting point and include others' situations as you are cultivating your ideal hosting event. By the time you have fully curated your idea, you will be ready to host others in a way that is deeply fulfilling and not just entertaining.

At this point you may be wondering, "how does someone become this passionate about hosting with a hospitable intent?" Truthfully, there are endless reasons why people are drawn to the idea and act of intentional hosting; but for me, this is deeply rooted in my faith. Today, we would refer to this sort of hospitality as *biblical hospitality*.

To help create a better picture of this, we're going to look at a few sections from *The Power of Biblical Hospitality* by Jeff Christopherson. Connection is the birthplace of love and good works, and biblical hospitality is what strengthens it. Biblical hospitality refers to one's decision to honor others and receive uplifting energy as it is reciprocated. It is the process of making people feel at home and welcomed within your space. I want to introduce to you Christopherson's ideas on the differences between the act of entertaining and the art of hospitality. So many times, we mistake the two for the same. Biblical hospitality differs from merely entertaining guests. Christopherson notes, "entertainment impresses; hospitality blesses." However, entertainment impresses at the surface and is short-lived, while hospitality "transcends time and style." True hospitality is the same now as it was in the Bible thousands of years ago. Let's talk about how and why that is. Christopherson offers four ways to further make the distinction between hospitality and entertainment. I have adapted his teachings into a four-step Vibe Check.

Before we jump in the steps, lets first explore what a vibe check is. Vibe is short for vibration. It's the energy that is in the room. You know what a bad vibe is because you feel uncomfortable and look around awkwardly. You know what a good vibe is too, where the conversation is flowing and the dynamic is good. Whether you're the host or the entertainer, you are always aware of the vibe in the room. It is your job to initiate and maintain it. It's important to you that your guests feel a good vibe so they are at ease. So, a vibe check is essentially you checking-in on the vibe throughout your time with them. Not only are you checking on the vibe in the atmosphere, but also with each person. Two people could have to completely different vibes, and it's really important to acknowledge this and be mindful of it. Throughout the event, simply check in with people and make sure that they're vibing at the right level.

We'll dive deeper into cultivating a vibe in just a little bit, but for now, it's only important that you begin to discern entertainment from hospitality using these four questions.

1. Who is the primary focus?
2. What is my purpose?
3. How is intimacy being fostered?

4. Where is the diversity and am I cultivating an inclusive space?

The questions are straight-forward, right? They are not designed to trick you, nor overcomplicate the art of hosting. In answering these questions, a host is better positioned to move from the role of an event coordinator, to the high vibration of stewardship.

Chapter Five

Step 1: Who is the Primary Focus?

Now that you have an understanding of the components of a vibe check, let's go a little deeper. The first question calls on the power of perspective or orientation. As hosts, it's quite easy to get swept up in the marvelous fog of wanting to impress. As pretentious and exaggerated as that sounds, it may actually be overflowing from the page and coming in your house because you know that as you are getting things prepared these are some of the thoughts you may or may not have had. If we are being honest with ourselves, we've all had similar thoughts to varying degrees. How many of us can admit to focusing on putting on display how "great" our life is compared to our guests by hosting the "perfect event" in our "perfect house" surrounded by our "perfect family" while suited and booted in our "perfect outfit" that fits our "perfect body." I get it. We come from a generation where *stuntin' is a habit*. Striving for perfection and the intent behind it could actually be trigger-ing to those who are on the receiving end. But a host with this mentality may be unconsciously positioning themself at cen-ter stage low-key evoking jealousy among their peers. Likely, this not your intention, but may be the impact if your focus is misplaced.

The seemingly innocent desire to impress others is in all ac-tuality a self-serving act. An act that manifests into superficial gatherings where the focus remains on the impressive nature of the host. Think about it. When you have just cleaned your house or prepared an amazing meal, you look forward to the complements about how you seemingly live life. There is this satisfaction that someone noticed enough to comment on it. You may feel this little feeling of triumph in your chest. However, the intent behind your hosting is not about showing others how we live life, but using what we have to enlighten their lives. When we focus on showing others how we live life, then we can fall into the habit of trying to stunt on others.

As great as this feeling may be, it's fleeting and superficial at best. There is limited satisfaction in *things*, especially when compared to actually community. Not only do you have these fleeting feelings, but your guests may be feeling things that are the opposite of the intended purpose for gathering. For example, instead of feeling happy to be around everyone, they may feel a little inadequate or resentful. This is definitely not how we want our guests to leave. There is no satisfaction in those feelings whatsoever.

Even if you are trying your best to make other people feel at home and are concerned about them, you probably are also concerned with how they perceive you in your subconscious. This is why you are at the center of attention according to modern day perceptions on hospitality. Things have to be "perfect" because they are a reflection of who? *You.* So, when the bathroom is messy or the food falls flat, you have this increased anxiety because you don't feel like your guest will be leaving giving you a 5-star rating. This type of pressure can be what makes hosting so stressful. Anxiety takes away from being able to really treat your guests to a good time and takes away from *why* you even decided to host a group of people you care about. This way of thinking would be characterized as "entertaining" because ultimately the "perception of you" is at the center of attention. Don't get me wrong - it is exceptional that you want to put forth so much effort to show people a good time. But check in with yourself. What is hosting doing to you physically, mentally, and spiritually?

You may answer this question saying, "I feel great!" and that may be true, but is it 100% honest? I will be the first to be transparent and can say, from personal experience, that I used to feel drained after hosting. I put so much effort into making sure that every detail was perfect. But, I was relieved when it was over. Of course, I would feel a little better if it went well. But if it didn't, then the pitfalls of that event would haunt me and roll over into any future considerations of having another event. This overflow of negative or disappointing outcomes from previous events just adds to the pile of worry for the next event. It's a never-ending cycle of all feelings that the Bible cautions against.

> "An anxious heart weighs a man down, but a kind word cheers him up." (Proverbs 12:25, NIV)

One of the rewarding parts of hosting and entertaining is when someone gives you compliments on how well it went for them. We all love to be boosted about how great the food was or how beautiful our homes or the décor was. Although these compliments make the worry and anxiety diminish just a little, we still are super relieved when the event is over. If anything I've described above hits close to home for you, then I encourage you to take the time to reflect on whether or not you may be at the center of attention for these events. You may be entertaining, under the guise of hospitality. Jeff Christopherson emphasizes the point that our guests should leave feeling enriched and encouraged from just being in our presence, not from your display of perfection.

When we put all of our focus on the appearance of everything, the opportunity to truly bless and fulfill the needs of guests can be overlooked. By adjusting the orientation, we're asking hosts to step out of the spotlight and instead shine it on each guest. This is the true meaning of hospitality. You are not simply trying to entertain people or show them how great your life is. You definitely aren't trying to make anyone jealous. You are trying to build community with others. Our main goal as intentional hosts, is to open the gate to bring others into a warm and inviting space putting them at the center of attention. Our mission is to ensure all those who enter our space feel enriched and encouraged by meaningful, intentional interactions.

As a host, you take on the primary duty of creating a sacred space that serves others, not boosting the ego. Sure, it feels nice. We all know that positive reinforcement can feel like a major payday for our self-image. However, Luke 14:11 tells us, "for all those who exalt themselves will be humbled, and those who humble themselves will be exalted." You are hosting to uplift your community, to bless others. By remembering this, we'll accomplish two things - we can both humble ourselves as well as elevate our guests in knowing who is at the center of attention.

So, when we consider who the center of attention is, we should ask ourselves to whom are we catering? The goal of intentional hosting is not simply to make your guests feel at home, but to have them feel like you thought about them. Are you feeding their soul? Are you providing them with something meaningful? Are you thankful for their presence and everyone's opportunities to fellowship with each other? This is the base of hosting with the intent of hospitality, which will be the focus for the rest of this chapter.

When I prepare for guests, whether they are visiting for just a few hours or staying overnight, I dedicate some time before their arrival to consider what my guests could've potentially sacrificed to spend time with me. I image the potential travel challenges parents of small children encountered while embarking on the trip to my home. Did they stay up all night packing, after putting the kids to bed, all just to get up at the crack of dawn to hit the road? For my good girlfriends that are coming to hangout, what kind of week did they have leading up to my event? Have I planned my activities in consideration of those challenges? For the parents, did I build in downtime for a much-needed time of rest? For my sister/friend who endured a grueling work week, did I create a moment to hear her heart and encourage her?

I hope as you're reading this chapter, you realize all the ways in which you can be the person that others need without overextending yourself. Even though the focus is not on you, you have to take care of yourself to preserve the longevity of meeting together. So, the questions above should give you an idea of how you can be there for people in the simplest manner. Hardworking adults and parents may just want a relaxing place to openly share about what is going on in their lives. Friends and family may have some things going on in their lives that you just have no clue about. This is a space for them to feel open enough to share that.

That's all hosting is. When we talked about hosting earlier, I mentioned several times that hosting doesn't have to be a huge, elaborate event. It can be, but the priority is to first establish genuine, intimate connections. It focuses on the needs of the community, as small or as big as they may be. Thus, the foundation of intentional hosting is to put yourself in others' shoes. This is where we can practice perspective - where you literally imagine yourself as your community member. Position yourself as if you were them and imagine their lives, demands, stressors, worries, and the like. Ask yourself what would you want and need to feel uplifted in their shoes.

> [8]Above all, keep loving one another earnestly, since love covers a multitude of sins. [9]Show hospitality to one another without grumbling. [10]As each has received a gift, use it to serve one another, as good stewards of God's varied grace. - 1 Peter 4: 8 -10(ESV)

This verse, too, touches on purpose, which we will get to soon; but the important part about this verse is showing hospitality without grumbling. This is what could be a shortcoming of entertainment. It takes so much energy, that it's hard to get through the planning and the event, without complaining about it. I am not a complainer. I'm a doer, but I'm probably going to let some complaints slip out here and there. It's not that I'm not grateful for the opportunity to host others, but it's taking so much of my energy, that it's hard to be as appreciative of the opportunity as I should be. I'm going to assume that I'm not alone in that boat…

This is where we can lean on hospitality. Hosting with the intention of hospitality is meant to be simple so we can steward one another without complaint. We can look forward to the joy and fulfilment that both my guests and I will leave with. Not only did we find time to come together, but we have this long-lasting satisfaction about the time we just spent together. Everyone leaves feeling better than they came, despite the fact that they may have to go right back into that same situation. Why? Because everyone has something unique to contribute - we each have gifts, specifically placed within us to help make a situation better.

As we near the end of this chapter, I hope your view on intentional hosting, or at least your thoughts on it, have started to change. I want to take away the perception that it is intimidating. Hosting can be much simpler, especially when you take a step back and consider who is at the center of attention. For a quick summary, remember, that "entertaining is about honoring the host" and "hospitality is about honoring the hosted." I encourage you, in your planning, to invite your guests to the center of the experience. Your thoughts should be about your guests and how you want them to leave feeling about themselves. This will help leave a long-lasting impact that won't dissipate as soon as they get back to reality.

Chapter Six

Step 2: What is My Purpose?

The things you are passionate about are not random,
they are your calling.
— Fabienne Fredickson

The second question is one of *purpose*. What is yours? We've got
so many things on our agenda. Most of you are working jobs
or building careers full-time. Some are raising children. Many
find time to volunteer or give back in some way. Whatever you
may personally have going on at the moment, the activities
that we engage in ask one common thing of you: you have
to be willing to step up and step out to accomplish anything.
Whether it's a permanent or temporary push, that may require
you to leave your comfort zone. You may have to dig up and
dust-off aspects of yourself that allow you to fulfill your roles
with efficacy.

The same can be said for hosting. Listen, I know how busy you
are. Perhaps with some or all of the roles I've just mentioned,
along with many more. Somehow in the midst of it all, you are
the one who tends to do the inviting and gathering of people
in your circles. Every time there is a milestone to be celebrated,
you put on your event planning hat and fulfill the role. Ac-

knowledging the important role that you play in your sacred communities, I am going to promote you. You are no longer a mere entertainer or event coordinator from this point forward. Your new title is even more appreciable than that of a host. As a representative of biblical hospitality, you have earned the title of *Community Cultivator*. This title signifies a deeper purpose than that of an entertainer. Recognize, that as a practice rooted in faith and divine possibility, hospitality serves the purpose of creating sacred space for others, breaking down barriers that exist between us, and strengthening bonds within our communities for the long-term. Now, *that* is a powerful purpose.

A Community Cultivator has a bigger role than an entertainer because there is some form of leadership that comes along with the role. You are the leader of planning and getting people together. Whatever your leadership style is, you are a leader. Now it's time to find ways to cultivate your leadership skills so that you are not the drained entertainer, but the empowered Community Cultivator.

I learned from a young age how important leadership is in bringing people together and hosting. I remember my very first job. It wasn't your typical fast-food job and it definitely was not at the typical age when a teenager starts to work. I am the daughter of two preachers, one of them a pastor. My first job was at the age of 9 or 10, collating papers for my dad's sermons on Sundays. His hand-written notes looked like works of art! The script was written like a beautiful font and I found the use of highlighters to categorize talking points mesmerizing. I remember being intrigued flipping through the multi-color highlighted pages, that often referenced concepts of how to be mindful of one another, kind to one another and how to encourage one another. At a very young age, my dad inspired my interests to learn all I could about leading people. I was probably the youngest person in school toting around Spencer Johnson' *Who Moved my Cheese?* When you grow up with both of your parents being leaders of different types of communities, you learn a lot about the role leadership plays in fostering community. Leaders are hosts. In my opinion, strong leaders are mindful of the dynamic that is created and fostered when they bring those that they are leading together. Strong community leaders create a space to inspire and motivate and demonstrate empathy where needed.

As the host, you take on a similar role of leaders that are commissioned to create safe spaces. I invite you to share in that same calling. Intentional hosting serves a great purpose. We all have a purpose. Knowing yours and the role you play positions us to show up mindfully and carry out the larger purpose- intentional connection. As someone who values my role as host, I am encouraged and empowered because gathering is truly a gift to one another. Being able to bring people together, and fulfill your purpose as a leader with the skills to make everyone around you feel very comfortable is a powerful purpose in its own right.

Purpose is something that is mentioned a lot in the Bible. In the context of our lives in general, purpose is why we are here on this earth and what we should do with our time. We were put here to do something, touch someone's life, pursue a mission, *something*. Most of the time, when we consider purpose, we think about it in a small context. When asked, our natural inclination is to start thinking about our careers and what we're going to do in life. That same consideration that you give purpose in regards to your life, is the same consideration that you should give purpose in regards to your social inter-action. We talked a little about why you are hosting in the last chapter, but that was for a different focus. This focus is purely about having the impact on people that can persist through life's various stages.

As a developer of community, let's really consider our purpose when hosting. Your purpose needs to serve three different peo-ple: you, your guests, and the will of God. In order to have the best hosting experience, there needs to be alignment in order to feel appreciated, listened to and encouraged.

So, let's start with your purpose as an intentional host and how you can step into it. Yes, we just took the time to discuss the importance of removing yourself from the spotlight. But at the end of the day, if you are taking hosting upon yourself, as a devoted cultivator and protector of the well-being of your community, then you will be affected in some way. You want to make sure that whatever this effect is, that it is a good and positive one. This will be positive reinforcement for you to keep extending the invitation and keep building community.

As the Community Cultivator, recognize that communities take time to establish. It is going to take a sequence of fulfill-ing events for you to start to see transformation and sense of connectedness develop among your loved ones. But the key to having this sequence of events is persistence. You have to continually seek ways to gather and connect people. Does this mean that every week you need to plan a get together for hundreds of people? No way. That's not sustainable and in many cases, not necessary by any means. Not even the experienced host would be able to be persistent or consistent with that tall of an order.

What it does mean, is finding small ways connect with people on a frequent basis. This could be as simple as asking a friend to coffee on a Saturday morning, and making this a regular date. If it doesn't work out one week, then simply reschedule and continue building that relationship. It's simple, but perhaps could grow into a consistent event attracting more people with similar interests. I would consider that manageable and the only thing you have to do is show up and be yourself. Two fairly simple things compared to the responsibilities of throwing large parties. The importance of the simplicity of hosting in this manner is that you are preserved. So even though their growth and spirit are the main focuses as you are considering joining together, your wellbeing is important too. Hosting is about uplifting everyone's spirit, including your own!

The goal of intentional hosting shouldn't be that it takes away a lot of time from your life and it definitely shouldn't leave you feeling drained. When you can relax and be yourself, then you have more energy to put towards sharing and listening to those around you. This is how community is built. As a community leader, at the core, you are responsible for creating the time and place for everyone to gather, creating a space for stories to be told and shared. While you're listening and speaking with others, people are also listening and speaking with you. Therefore, everyone in attendance can get the same nurturing and encouragement, by connecting into the spirit, that they need to go back to their lives and continue pushing forward.

This will be very important as we come out of isolation, racial tensions, and all the other soul striking events of this year. Come up with a place and time for people to meet to talk about their issues and how to renew their spirit and faith and just show up. Maintain this space for people to continue meeting and sharing, and be amazed at the growth and development in your very own community all because you removed the weighted focus on the elements that may not have the highest impact and made sure not to overwhelm yourself with the intricacies and stressors of entertainment.

The second entity to consider when thinking about your purpose is your guest. Although we have talked briefly about how we want our guests to feel when leaving, it's important to zone in on our purpose when it comes to others. So, while considering your purpose for others when hosting an event, understand that your purpose may change. Quite often, actually. It depends on what's happening and why you are hosting an event. For example, as you are thinking about hosting people during the current climate, your purpose may be creating a safe space (physically and emotionally) for people to talk about their experiences. Creating a safe space may take a little more work and creativity on your part, but it should be something fairly simple that you set up and don't think about anymore so you can revert your attention back to what really matters. As the community leader, you may have more precautions that you need to consider when creating the safe space because you want your guests to feel comfortable so they can be vulnerable.

Creating a safe space includes thinking about the current climate of things. Do your guests feel safe psychologically, physically, emotionally? Once again, your purpose is to be mindful of your environment and create a space where people feel comfortable talking about the things they are going through. Are your guests the only ones that look like them in the group? Are they in a hostile environment that will not allow them to truly express how they are feeling? These are things you have to consider and realize that as the community leader, your purpose may be to foster this inviting environment. This shouldn't be something stressful, but just something to be mindful of. This is being aware of your guests and putting their needs in the center. Just focusing on your comfort level and who you feel encouraged by without considering how other guests may feel, detracts from empathetic hospitality.

Another thing to consider when thinking about your purpose towards others is how do you want them to feel transformed after meeting with you? Once again, this will change, especially depending on who you have around you. Going back to the idea of different communities, each one will have a different makeup of people. Therefore, your purpose when bringing together one group may not be the same when you're with another group. Hosting is not a one-size-fits-all task. This is why it's important to be present. You aren't just slapping on one method of hosting every time you host, regardless of who's around. You incorporate those questions that we've talked about that center around why you're hosting and what you want your guests to feel when they leave. From there, cultivate the right vibe for that group.

This idea of how they feel transformed also touches on the entertaining vs. hosting discussion that we just had. If you are entertaining, then the transformation of your guests may be short lived and mixed with some more negative feelings like jealously and resentment. Hosting, on the other hand, should aim to positively impact and encourage your guests. After they leave your presence, they should feel renewed and thankful to have spent that time. Since hosting is an ebb and flow of energy, you may also feel the same way after hosting the event. Being mindful of others and their ability to return feelings of empathy and concern is a mutually beneficial exchange.

Finally, the last, but certainly not least, entity that we may need to think about when considering our purpose is God or being grateful for the gifts that we possess. How is our hosting fulfilling God's promises and expectations for us or how are we fully utilizing our strengths? Throwing a fancy party is not doing either of these things to their full potential. If your event focuses more on how others can bring glory to you, then you also may not be fulfilling your purpose to God or to your talents.

As you consider hosting and have figured out how to make it sustainable for your wellbeing and relevant to the lives of your guest, what's left is figuring out how to pursue the purpose that God gave you while hosting, or taking full advantage of your set of skills. God has blessed each and every one of us with skills, materials, wealth, gifts, or resources to properly host people and bring them closer to Him. We have something in our possession that others don't. How are you going to use these unique things, gifts and qualities to help you fulfill your purpose? These are thoughts to consider in the name of intentional hosting.

If you're having a hard time and not feeling like you have a lot to offer, but still want to host, take a moment to consider what you have. Take an inventory of skills, books, experiences, your home, transportation, donatable items or money, anything that could help change the life of another. You can use any one of those things, or several of them, to host and fulfill your purpose. You don't have to give so much of yourself away that you can't sustain your role as community leader, but use what God has given you in a way to be a vessel of knowledge and a walking demonstration of what consistent faith and prayer can do for those around you.

So, now thinking about what we have just discussed, I want to lay it out in a very clear manner so you know exactly what questions to ask yourself regarding purpose and hosting. The first one is, how can I fulfill my purpose of being a good community leader? This question will allow you to start thinking about all the good you could do in your community by simply being a good host. This question will cause you to think about what you have to do to be an effective and intentional host. How can you host something on a consistent basis, so the forsaking of gathering doesn't happen, while making sure you, too, feel spiritually satisfied instead of drained? How can your purpose serve you just as much as it serves the people around you? When planning to host, grandeur may take away from how you could benefit, and add to how you could suffer. These are things that we need to reconsider. Why are you doing them and what will be the consequences if you don't? If the consequences are more about how you will look than what will happen to your faith or spirit, then understand it's an entertainment factor that can be done without.

The second question, what is my purpose to others? Remember, the answer to this is ever changing because it depends on who "others" is. Your overall purpose will have to do with recognizing the needs of that specific community and meeting them. Hosting should leave you both feeling like you are completely encapsulated by love and attention, something that's quite difficult to attain when you are overburdened with logistics.

The last question is, how can I reach my purpose while honoring God or being thankful for my talents? Hosting isn't about stretching yourself thin or pretending to be someone you're not. It's about being a testimony of what God has blessed you with, or the skills that you possess, and then using them to bless others. If you have a talent, but aren't using it to transform the lives of others, then you are not utilizing it to its full potential. Regardless of how futile or small you think your talent is, you have it. So how are you going to give it? What better way of using it than letting it be the main driving force behind your method of hosting?

Think about these questions when you are hosting and they will help you reach your purpose and give you something to think about. It's easier to stay focused on the task at hand when you are constantly reminding yourself of what your purpose is. Throughout the planning and execution, keep coming back to your answers to these questions and they will help you stay anchored when the logistics and stressors of hosting threaten to swoop down and carry you away.

Pause and Reflect

Let's work a bit with the concept of purpose. I made reference to a quote from Fabienne Fredrickson:

> "The things you are passionate about are not random, they are your calling."

This quote sheds light upon a fundamental aspect of our lives. What we are passionate about isn't random. It is all a part of the plan laid out for us by the universe. Our purpose lies in our passions and is carried out in the people we interact with.

1. Take a moment to brainstorm and jot down some things that energize you.
2. How do you incorporate these into your daily lives?

Chapter Seven

Step 3: How is Intimacy Fostered?

Connection is the energy that is created between
two people when they feel seen, heard, and valued –
when they can give and receive without judgement.
— Brene Brown, PhD, LMSW

Let's move on to the third question. This brings us to the topic
of intimacy, and perhaps more importantly, how we go about
fostering it. When we think about our healthiest relationships,
platonic or otherwise, what is true about them? Both parties
create and hold safe space for the sharing of personal truths.
Partners devote time to learning about their needs, concerns,
insecurities, and passions. Within intimate relationships, people make time to learn new things and collect new experiences
together. People also have to pause, take the time to assess their
own role in a relationship, and periodically assess the fit of the
relationship as it progresses. Does it still...*make sense*?

As a community builder or leader, you will carry a set of similar
responsibilities to cultivate a space where genuine intimacy can
grow. Creating intimacy for your guests and throughout your
gathering is not about filling moments with self-centered conversation to impress others. Biblical hospitality is not meant to
be a platform to brag and boast about all the wonderful things
occurring in your life. Certainly, it's acceptable to share your

blessings with others and be an example of what it means to be the recipient of God's abundant love. However, biblical hospitality is about expanding that focus outward; inviting others to occupy the spotlight. It's about opening a space for others to engage in meaningful conversation about their joys, sorrows, dreams, accomplishments, and whatever other topics may be on their heart to share. As an intentional host, your duty is to display a willingness to listen.

As social beings, we often connect through storytelling. Every time you catch a family member up on how life has been since you last spoke, or describe your future plans to a friend, you're engaging in storytelling. It's really that simple! At first glance, leaning into one another in this way appears to be nothing more than a harmless conversation, especially because it happens naturally. Yet as you may have guessed, there's a deeper conversation around this just waiting to be unpacked! We can recognize that storytelling often encourages humans to try to one-up each other; to tell a better, more engaging version of whatever the last person added to the conversation. We all know that person who listens to someone speak, only to interject saying something along the lines of, "You think that's crazy? Wait until you hear what happened to me!" Or maybe you know someone who tries a little too hard to fill empty silences with stories to wow the group. These types of responses are usually not carried out with malicious intent, yet the impact can be monumental in terms of the message it sends to your guest: this is about me, and you're only here to fuel my ego. As you'd assume, this is not what fostering intimacy seeks to convey.

We're here to invite others to the center. To share that space with those who need their voices amplified and heard in the particular moment you hold together. This act of asking meaningful questions, and graciously lending an ear to others is referred to as *holding space*. Imagine if you went to visit a doctor and the doctor spent your whole appointment telling you about their health conditions and ailments. Or, what happens if the server at your favorite restaurant dominates the conversation by telling you what they like to eat, thereby ignoring your wants, needs, and time? You'd likely be uncomfortable, perhaps frustrated, and frankly, quite confused. Take hosting as your opportunity to protect your guests from feeling those feels. Building intimacy is the way for you to guide the energy circulating through your event from superficial to spiritual. True hosting forms a relationship. So, tend to it as such!

First, what exactly is intimacy? When people consider intimacy, they usually think of the act as simply being close to someone, specifically in a romantic context. Although romantic relationships involve the cultivation of intimacy, intimacy itself can actually be applied to any sort of relationship. If we move our thoughts beyond romance, intimacy is simply knowing another person deeply and feeling like they know you deeply as well. When we look at intimacy in this manner, we are able to apply it to any close connections we have with others like friends, family, mentors and other types of interactions.

We can also define intimacy as a close, familiar and affectionate or loving personal relationship with another person or group. True intimacy is fostered by having a deep awareness of another person's *being*. In carrying that awareness of how someone may be thinking, feeling, or behaving in a particular moment, you create a space for others to be themselves. When one feels seen, heard and acknowledged in the absence of judgement, the barriers that would otherwise deter us from relaxing into the moment begin to dissolve. When you create a space where people feel secure enough to present their authentic self, you're offering a level of genuine closeness that is rather scarce in many circles today.

This expanded way of acknowledging intimacy reveals greater depths of companionship or togetherness. We can now apply those principles to several different aspects of our lives and different types of relationships. With these new ideas on just what this level of closeness is, we can, once again, open up the ways that we apply them in our lives. Now, when you think about your close friendships, or support groups, you can use some of the concepts we discuss in this chapter to strengthen and deepen those bonds even more.

When we discussed community in Chapter 3, we unpacked several types. Moving forward, we'll explore how a multi-variant framework also holds true for intimacy. The ways in which we spend time together, as well as the aspects of our lives that we choose to delve deeper into, differ across groups of people. Factors such as personality type, deep-rooted beliefs, and even past experiences can influence how one demonstrates or accepts intimacy. For example, introverted personalities are likely to take more time to open up and only do so with a select few, but many appreciate deep levels of intimacy once a fair amount of rapport is built. Without rapport, an introvert will likely stay to themselves. On the other hand, extroverts enjoy touching base with everyone! That also means many interactions sort of skim the surface instead of diving deep. Introverts value comfort and depth. Extroverts value variety and breadth. Giving thought to how these factors, the nature of your roles throughout your community, and any other variables that influence how intimacy currently shows up in your world are keys to cultivating more impactful interactions. As you continue to enrich your perception of intimacy, I encourage you to consider the ways intimacy is created and displayed throughout your unique connections.

Now, let's jump right into the various types of intimate connections. The first that we will discuss is *experiential intimacy*. This is when people are bound together by leisure activities. They find themselves acting the same way as others when they are all participating in similar works. Teamwork is a good example of this type of togetherness. When people work together to accomplish a certain goal and their moves take on this synchronous activity, that by itself is fostering a deeper level of mutuality. Everyone is working together towards a common accomplishment. Therefore, everyone's actions have to be coordinated. This requires a certain level of hearing and being heard so that everyone can contribute to the group in a similar fashion.

Some examples of experiential intimacy are things like game nights, movie dates and happy hours. Everyone comes together with these common interests to have a good time with one another. This is a fun and loose environment in which people are able to open up and get to know one another. These don't take a lot of work, just some organization; but the benefits can be immeasurable. As the root word gives away, experiential intimacy is all about channeling the energy of a common *experience* into a special moment of connection.

We talked previously about making plans, but not following through because life gets in the way. Occasions built around experiential intimacy help eliminate resistance and encourage follow-through. These are activities that can be executed with minimal planning from the host. For example, planning a group outing may only require something as simple as collecting RSVPs and making a reservation. It's easy to imagine how enjoyable a simple gathering like this could be for everyone involved, especially during these times. It just takes a few people to commit to a time and a place, then let the uplifting vibes draw everyone into the precious moment!

Another common place we can find experiential intimacy is church and other types of spiritual gatherings. As someone who finds the church to be an essential part of my well-being, I can tell you that I look forward to gathering with others over our shared faith each service. Whether in-person or virtual, the level of experiential intimacy that spiritual gatherings bring is refreshing. Throughout the week, it's easy to lose sight of how we connect to others in a meaningful way. But when we dedicate time to sit in fellowship with one another and receive God's word, the experience ties us together. There's no you. There's no me. It's just us and God's unconditional love, bound together.

The next form of intimacy is **emotional intimacy**. This type is achieved when people feel at peace with being vulnerable. It's about creating an environment where others feel comfortable and safe enough to express their personal wants, needs and feelings. Often times, it can be very difficult to open up to even the closest of friends and family. However, creating this bubble where people can share their thoughts without fear of judgement or dismissal will make it possible to disclose even the most uncomfortable of sentiments. Now, this is not a type of relationship that can be developed with just anyone. It takes time to build up the trust to share these thoughts with family members and very close friends. However, once you are at that point with someone, that is a deeper connection that allows you both to feel acknowledged and valued.

Emotional intimacy is an incredible type of rapport. The most solid relationships of any kind are held together by individuals who are committed to expressing personal truths while also allowing space to engage with another's. This doesn't mean you should be consumed by other people's "stuff." At it's very best, emotional intimacy flows as a two-way street. It's about knowing *how* to listen and *when* to share. Every time there is this secure exchange of personal matter, the bond between you and the other person continues to grow stronger.

Considering the nature of emotional conversations, the spaces where these types of exchanges happen would potentially take place in a more formal, private, or secure setting. Be mindful of your space when the circumstances allow. If you're creating the space for someone to unpack a recent hardship or someone has offered to do the same for you, what environment is most conducive to offering support? Of course, many factors go into determining any specifics. But staying mindful of how external elements surrounding the conversation, such as noise level, impact the interaction will take you far. This may require some level of pre-planning depending on the situation at hand. However, don't run from this if it's been placed on your heart. If a bit of proper planning makes the difference between attempting to build emotional intimacy in the middle of a crowded restaurant, versus mindfully creating a space built for comfortable exchange; any additional efforts will not be in vain.

While the types of gatherings that promote emotional intimacy may take a little more work, they don't have to become a huge production that may eventually take a toll on you. If you would like to go all out on an event to make people feel very welcome, go ahead and do your thing! But just know that something simple and low-key can also lead to a beneficial outcome. Speaking of outcomes, remember your role isn't to become the community therapist. Nor are you being asked to put on a shiny cape and save everyone from their personal struggles. Again, emotional intimacy is all about holding space for one another to be at peace within themselves. Not everyone is looking for a solution or to be "fixed." People just want permission to feel and to still be accepted while doing so.

Intellectual intimacy is the third and final type that we will discuss. Although, there are several other types of intimacy that are beyond the scope of this book and I encourage you to further explore on your own if you find yourself interested in learning more. Intellectual intimacy involves getting to know more about how people think. It's a collaborative space for individuals to come together and share what's on their minds. Even if people disagree and can appropriately express their opposition, these get-togethers get the blood flowing in the brain as thought exchanges potentially influence the perspective of those in attendance.

Conversations and exchanges that stimulate the mind are a predominant theme in these events. They don't have to be conversations about personal information, but personal opinions on things happening around you. Dinner parties and networking events are some great options for cultivating this type of atmosphere. These types of events are a means of bringing individuals together in a collaborative sense. The overarching goal is to connect ideas and interests that are compatible and/or benefit the entirety of the group.

Why is it important that you are involved in the engaging aspects of your event? Because building this sense of closeness or fostering any type of intimacy, has some important benefits that you should experience as well as your guests. One of these benefits is providing that sense of belonging that we talked about in the first chapter. When people are a part of tribes, they feel as if they have an identity or association with a particular group of people. This is very important for people's sense of self. And your guest's sense of self is not the only one that matters. Just because you are the organizer, doesn't mean that you shouldn't get to feel this sense of belonging either. Sometimes it's easy to feel on the outside when you're busy hosting and taking care of logistics while everyone else gets to focus solely on engaging with others. You may miss out on some of the thoughtful interactions that are happening and strengthening this sense of connection. Although you are facilitating the event, be extra cognizant that you, too, are participating in these powerful moments.

The powerful moments are the ones that make people feel truly connected when brought together. Without this level of inter-action, the elements that make tribe are lacking. The energy may start to feel more like a group of people who happen to be in proximity of one another, but have not accessed a deeper bond. It becomes very transactional. What makes the differ-ence between this and a fruitful social circle, is that there is this level of affection and reciprocity between the members of the group. There's a secure connection that remains as such because while one pours into another, the other remains ready to receive and reciprocate that energy. This feeling of closeness to other individuals who are experiencing something similar to you is a deeply satisfying feeling. When you can feel seen and heard by people who care for you and willingly offer that back in return, no one is alone. Even when life is just not going your way, you still know that you have a solid support group which can bring more comfort than one may realize. The benefits of building these bonds between different people in your life are overwhelmingly positive. However, it does not always come easy. There are many intimacy issues that the host, in partic-ular, may inadvertently face. It's important to recognize and deconstruct these issues so that you are free to host how you feel is best without any hang ups.

A common emotional block is the feeling that one should have or should be a better friend. Many of us have been here before. We get so caught up in what we've got going on, that we forget to make that phone call or we have to reschedule that date.

It's normal to feel some form of guilt about not upholding all of your promises or putting your issues in front of spending time with friends and family. However, it's life and it happens to all of us. No one is perfect and sometimes we aren't able to connect with our friends to the level that we feel like we should. What's more important is recognizing when a connection needs to be tended to, then taking action on that feeling. If you continuously push aside the fact that you haven't spent time bringing people together for some sort of exchange or participating, then that's when we have to reevaluate how to fit that community into our lives.

Another aspect of hosting to remain mindful of is the balance between having an active social life and actually being in genuine connection with someone. You may know a lot of people and spend time with them, but without the intentional conversations that have the goal of building a deeper bond, then you may be missing out on those benefits of connection. A reluctancy to be vulnerable with those around us will keep us from reaching that level of intimacy that will push us to the next level with certain individuals.

Many people struggle with vulnerability. From a cultural perspective, perhaps vulnerability has become synonymous for weak or being too emotional. Yet in all actuality, being vulnerable requires massive courage! It's a type of exposure that asks you to show up with complete transparency while not knowing what the outcome is going to be. Author and speaker, Brene Brown, shares that a client of hers once described vulnerability as "saying I love you for the first time." As humans we're designed to think and feel and while it's natural to want to share those thoughts and emotions with someone, there may be invisible barriers that prevent this sharing from happening naturally. Perhaps allowing yourself to be vulnerable does come easily, in which case the need to suppress inner emotions or live extremely guarded does not resonate with you. That is a blessing and I encourage you to recognize how your energy could benefit someone else who may not be quite there yet.

When we talk about how intimacy is fostered, we have to be honest about the fact that it isn't always something that happens instantly. When we were children, we could go to the park, play on the swings with someone for ten minutes and they were our new best friends. But the older some of us get, the stronger that "no new friends" mentality kicks in and the less likely we are to form new bonds. It's hard to trust that everyone you meet will align with your mission and that's where practicing discernment comes in. True intimacy isn't about giving all of your attention to everyone who wants it. Rather, it's about exercising discernment and showing up intentionally to garner that sort of deep trust between one another.

Intimacy is developed over time. Time is the critical factor to creating those meaningful relationships with others. Without time, it is hard to really get to know someone and decide if that's someone with whom you want a deeply connected relationship. The concept of time in this instance is not just about the length of time, but also the frequency. You have to take it upon yourself to partner with that other person and create environments for you to get close to one another. Do things that both of you really enjoy so you can create the foundation to build up upon.

Part of creating that atmosphere for bringing you closer to another individual is making sure that everyone feels safe. Emotional, physical, and psychological safety is an important component for bringing people together and moving beyond the surface with them. A psychologically-safe setting is one where people feel encouraged to take interpersonal risks, which looks like offering new ideas or challenging decisions for the sake of potentially arriving at a more favorable outcome. For example, if you've ever worked at a job where management was hostile, defensive, or not receptive to the needs, desires, or ideas of an employee, you've likely experienced the symptoms of a psycho-logically unsafe environment. Psychological safety promotes the acceptance of diverse thoughts. Over time, people become confident offering up their unique contributions because there is no fear of being punished, excluded or humiliated.

Anytime two or more people gather, the combined potential is limitless! That is if, and only if, there's room for free-flowing thoughts without harsh judgement. Even if people have oppos-ing views on the same topic, there's something for both parties to learn if they're willing to explore. We aren't all supposed to think the same. If we did, how much progress would we make as a collective? We do, however, have to honor our truths while allowing others to do the same. There are limits and boundar-ies to respect, of course. Prioritizing the fundamentals- trust, acceptance, honesty, safety, compassion, affection and good communication when creating a supportive environment will also help maintain the energy we'd want from such interactions.

"The problems arise simply when there is a mismatch between the level of social connection desired and the level the environment provides." – John T. Cacioppo and William Patrick, *Loneliness: Human Nature and the Need for Social Connection.*

As we bring our discussion of intimacy to a conclusion, let the sentiment shared above sit with you. Hosts carry the responsibility of reading the vibes in the room and making sure guests feel comfortable enough to arrive at a level of intimacy that makes them feel *whole* in your presence. It can be challenging to be aware of your guests when you have to devote your attention to details and tending to the intimacy of your gathering. We do the best we can to juggle the two, but I encourage you to preserve most of your energy for bringing people together in a meaningful way. Remember, "People would much rather have your attention, than your perfection." – Katie Deckert.

Pause and Reflect

1. Let's take a moment and be honest with ourselves. Have you ever found yourself trying to "one-up" another person in your tribe?

2. In what ways have you noticed this manifest - through conversation, materials, or anything else?

3. If we can explore a little deeper - why do you think you, or anyone for that matter, has a tendency to do this?

4. Before coming along on this intentional hosting journey with me, think about what "intimacy" meant to you. How would you have defined it?

5. Now, think about what you have learned after reading

Chapter 7. I talk about three different types of intimacy. Where do you find them fitting into the way you cultivate friendships? How can you, as a host, benefit from each?

6. When people feel out of place or overlooked, they move into their figurative shell and from that place, may feel disconnected from the community. As a host, how can you make sure your gathering(s) allows for each community member to feel important and valued?

7. This question may be relevant for some people, if not all. Can you recall a time in your life where you felt like the odd person out at an event?

   a. What emotions were triggered by this?

   b. How did you cope with those emotions?

   c. How could the host of that event made it more inclusive for everyone to connect?

Chapter Eight

Step 4: Am I Fostering Inclusion?

Remember what it felt like to be excluded so that
you can help to build a community where everyone
is included.
— Lisa Friedman

The fourth and final part of your vibe check shifts the focus to
inclusion. Do you know the feeling of walking into a room full
of strangers? This environment will provoke different feelings
depending on whether you identify with a more introverted or
extroverted personality, but maybe your palms are a bit sweaty
from being in an unfamiliar environment. You may have to
work through levels of nervousness until you adjust to new
faces and the echoes of unexplored voices. Although many
thought-provoking conversations may be within earshot, that
awkward moment in deciding how and when to contribute,
your voice stalls any action. For these reasons and many others, some people struggle with networking. If the struggles
associated with networking don't resonate with you, you're
blessed. However, you probably know at least one person, or
many, who do. For that reason, cultivating an inclusive space
where guests feel welcomed and at ease is a responsibility of
the host.

Let me be clear. It certainly isn't your job to sniff out everyone
with a social anxiety, give a diagnosis, and provide a treatment

in effort to achieve inclusion. In fact, please don't attempt to do so. You'll receive a handful of weird looks and make a lot of people uncomfortable! However, you do want to make a concerted effort to include your guests. You've already checked the vibe to ensure it is suitable for relational intimacy. The final part of your vibe check is about inviting others into that intimate space so that they may present themselves with authenticity. It is only when we move with authenticity that real love and connection can flow. From a place of authenticity, people feel comfortable being vulnerable. This is a wonderful thing!

I've referenced the work of Brene Brown in previous chapters. If you're not already familiar with the name, you'll want to be! Explore her work. Brown has spent nearly two decades researching vulnerability, shame, worthiness, and courage. Her work has touched millions of individuals and helped revive countless businesses alike as society searches for ways to enrich our connections in hopes of social progress. Brown encourages us to view vulnerability as a three-part mixture: uncertainty, risk, and emotional exposure. As we know, the word vulnerability itself often intimidates people. Maybe we're not quite clear on what it means, or how to live it out. Perhaps we've been conditioned to believe vulnerability is synonymous for *weak* and those outdated beliefs still linger. Let's change that perception for ourselves and others.

What if I told you there is no such thing as courage without uncertainty, risk, and emotional exposure? Yes, you read that right. These are the same three components of vulnerability! It is virtually impossible to have one without the other. Courage and vulnerability literally depend on each other. The type of genuine love and support that we've focused on is rather uncommon to come across for many. Some people haven't found their way to offer it. Others may not be in a position to receive it. Just as it is the case with many life challenges, it's easier to stay in the comfort zone. That's why your role as an intentional host or community leader takes courage. You are taking strategic and honest actions to influence the present interests and future prosperity of your community; while also acknowledging your limited ability to predict or control actual outcomes. You have the courage to show up for others by inviting them in. At the same time, your exposure to the many unknowns associated with that invitation allow you to feel vulnerable. See how that works? Courage and vulnerability - one doesn't exist without the other and they both present elements of uncertainty, risk, and exposure.

Courage and vulnerability bring us back to the call for inclusive spaces. Since we know vulnerability doesn't come easily for many, it's on us as hosts to create spaces where guests can shine authentically. True hospitality is about breaking down the barriers that block our tolerance for uncertainty, risk, and emotional exposure. When one feels safe enough to present their "self" in the truest sense, vulnerability is inherently present. From that vulnerable space, a mutually-rewarding connection can form where individuals feel important, validated, and valued.

The extent to which these feelings exist is what determines how inclusive a space really is at its core. Gathering in a space where your importance and value are validated by others feels noticeably different than occupying a space where you are overlooked and disregarded, right? Offer your guests the gift of hospitality by mindfully cultivating an environment where people aren't left wondering where they stand in relation to others. The powerful vibration of inclusion will become evident in conversation, activities and the overall flow of energy throughout whatever space you choose to host within. That's the kind of vibe you want circulating through anything your name is on!

The first question that we will explore together is what is *inclusion*? We may have a surface level understanding that it has something to do with making sure that everyone feels included. Most likely, most of us can recall a time when we weren't included or felt like someone else wasn't included, but we didn't know how to go about correcting that. Simply put, inclusion means that all people, regardless of their differences have the right to be respected and appreciated as valuable members of their communities. Everybody has a fair basis to contribute to the environment.

Consider this. Have you ever been out with people and wanted to speak, but kept getting interrupted or dismissed? Did that make you feel like you were a part of the group or like you just wanted to climb back into your shell until the event was over? I've definitely been there before and it's not a fun place to be. So, the best thing we can do as hosts is try to make sure that others don't feel this way. This includes some of what we talked about earlier with creating environments where everyone feels comfortable enough to share their thoughts, no matter how many levels of diversity there are. It is important to draw a connection between growing a bond and making people feel like they are contributing members, regardless of their role in the group.

The goal is to create a sense of belonging, because this puts people in a position to truly feel worthy by just being their true self. Few forms of satisfaction compare to the feeling of knowing you belong to a group that cares about you. From birth, humans naturally rely on a secure bond with others. When people are hesitant about pursuing acceptance in different groups, it may be because they have been in situations, previously, where they were excluded, judged, or experienced something else negative. As a host, your responsibility is not to be "The Fixer, " but instead to carry the energy that erases exclusion.

Creating inclusive spaces results in positive outcomes, both in the now and in the future. When people belong to a group, they become more self-aware. Ironic, isn't it? Whether explicitly expressed or indirectly implied, people can influence the ways we see ourselves. For example, college students go off to school for months at a time, collect new relationships and experiences, then return home months later to their original tribe. Let's say this college student happened to choose a top "party school." While they may have enjoyed a carefree, perhaps reckless lifestyle in school, returning to the loved ones that nurtured them may encourage a shift in behavior even if it is temporary. Of course, this fictional student could dive right back into the cycle of "party, sleep, party" once returning to school, but simply being in the presence of loved ones is enough to remind them of how certain actions or decisions may be perceived by others.

I don't use that example to suggest we should all be living our lives for other people. That's no way to live! However, it highlights the very real influence someone else's presence can have. We become mirrors for one another revealing and reflecting insights that lead to greater self-awareness. This dynamic triggers motivation within us. A family member's request to visit may finally be the motivation one needs to clean out the spare bedroom they've been using to store items that no longer serve a purpose. People tap into a higher level of effort when they're reminded that others are still aware of their existence. As a host, you are that reminder. Without seeking approval, you are also in a position to be reminded of just how valid your unique presence is as well. It's an "I see you seeing me, and I'll remain mindful of my presence so that I may affirm yours" type of thing!

Viewing interpersonal connections through that lens helps to remove the ego which often manifests into an "I" vs. "them" mindset. When the truth is, there would be no concept of either if it weren't for the other. There is no "I." There is no "them." There is only an "us"! Dis-ease occurs when worldly distractions obscure the truth and cause us to lose sight of our interconnectedness.

Consider what it feels like to be neglected in a partnership of any kind. The partner that feels neglected believes that they are owed something which will eventually turn into resentment if left unaddressed. What do you imagine happening if someone has an ongoing need that sits unfulfilled? They'll either leave or choose to stay. Yet if they stay, the person who feels neglected is likely to "check out," either mentally, emotionally, physically or all of the above.

If asked, most would say they would never want to intentionally neglect the feelings or desires of others. However, unless we exercise a heightened sense of awareness for how our presence affects others, it's easy to overlook the signals others put out. These are considerations to keep at the forefront of your mind as you invite others in. The more skilled you become at creating inclusive spaces that edify, the greater your community will benefit now and later.

Usually when we talk about inclusion, the concept of diversity isn't far. This is no coincidence! Inclusion on its own isn't quite complete. Adding diverse layers of thoughts, beliefs, backgrounds and much more is what ignites new possibilities. While we're all connected as one, we've also been gifted with diversity. Diversity allows us to personalize our experience; making our lives compatible with others, yet unlike anyone else. When we gather, it's important to realize how elements of diversity transform the quality of our interactions. We must leverage our people's unique and diverse natures as a means of establishing robust futures for generations to come. Significant developments are possible wherever there's tolerance for perspectives that don't all look the exact same.

What I mean by this is inclusion and belonging are two different sides of the same coin when it comes to increasing the diversity of a group. Inclusion is a choice. One quote by Dr. Britt Andreatta, in *Beyond Diversity: The Science of Inclusion and Belonging*, encompass the idea that as the host, we have some control over how to foster these types of environments. "Belonging is the feeling of being part of something and mattering to others. We create it through inclusion, which consists of intentional acts".

You can choose to encourage thought sharing of all your guests. If you notice someone is being talked over or judged, you can make the decision to take control of the conversation so you can give them the floor. These are all things that are within your control. What is not in your control, is their sense of belonging. That's what important to them feeling like they can share openly. Without that sense of comfort that comes with acceptance, your guests may be more reluctant to sharing and being open. This can detract from the sense of community and intimacy you are trying to foster. This is where we bring everything together. Your efforts of creating an alliance contribute to their feelings of feeling connected, which over time, can foster intimacy to build community. However, if you are lacking inclusion and belonging, then you may not be able to tap into the full potential of having a diverse crowd. There are so many benefits to having several different minded people together, but if they all don't feel comfortable sharing, then you may once again, only get to experience the thoughts and feelings of those very similar to you. This isn't necessarily a bad thing, but it does limit your experience, as well as everyone else's in attendance.

If you've kept up until this point, that tells me you're committed to upgrading your role of a host from an entertainer in pursuit of external validation and attention to an agent of change within your tribe, village or community. Altogether, the purpose of the four-step *Vibe Check* is to reframe your thoughts about welcoming others into your space before you invite them in. The *Vibe Check* is a practical way to align your thoughts, emotions and actions with the principles of biblical hospitality.

As we move forward, remember that our actions are rooted in faith, stewardship and community-building. We are working together to move ourselves away from the superficial act of entertaining others. You're not an actor tasked with putting on a show for others. You're a product of divine creation, and you're here to create deeper acts of love! Entertainment is for *my* benefit. Hosting is for my guests' benefit.

Now that you've got that down, continue on this journey with me where you will learn more than you realized to be true about a vibe as well as actionable steps towards reinforcing positive energy throughout your community.

Section Three
It's a Whole Vibe

Energy is contagious, positive and negative alike.
I will forever be mindful of what and who I am
allowing into my space.
— Alex Elle

Chapter Nine

Understand It.

Vibes speak louder than words.

We talk about vibes all the time. Before you commit to an invitation somewhere, you need to know, *"what's the vibe*?*"* We even recognize vibes at work, whether in an office setting or working virtually. It's no wonder we see workplaces increasingly acknowledge the importance of organizational culture. Efforts to build and maintain a workplace culture essentially create the vibe that influences your workday. When the vibe is good or neutral, it may go unnoticed. Yet, when the vibe is off, it's an obvious distraction.

People, most certainly, have and give off vibes. After talking with someone for a few moments, most of us are skilled enough to put language around the vibe that person gives off. Were they uplifting or more of a downer? Perhaps their energy came off a bit aggressive or maybe even cynical. What's interesting about vibes is while one person may be carrying it, the actual vibration that one sends off can virtually impact everyone and everything they come in contact with. For that reason, unlocking the truth behind vibes is a major key in growing your skillset as an intentional host. We're talking about the invisible, yet pervasive energy circulating through time and space wherever we gather.

You'll want to know what's going on behind the scenes so you can work your magic!

The term "vibe" is actually short for vibration. If you can recall learning about sound or light, you'll remember both of these things are concepts of energy. We know this because they're measured in waves, or frequencies, on the electromagnetic spectrum. We're most familiar with radio frequencies, which connect energy waves from the radio station to the stereo system in your car or home. We can't see them, but they exist right before us. We also know that light travels much faster than sound; about 877,193 times faster to be specific. We'll revisit this fact later.

Just like sound, light, and radio, our bodies have ways of transmitting energy, too. Our bodies are filled with energy waves, and this is by God's design. As we move through this world, we touch others with that energy, whether we mean to or not. The most important thing to grasp about human energy within the context of hosting is what we know to be true about frequencies. The higher the frequency, the higher the energy. If your internal energy vibrates at a higher frequency, then your energy is that much stronger to radiate. As an intentional host, it's necessary to be aware of how subtle energies throughout your gathering influence the dynamic.

To make vibrations a little easier to conceptualize, let's break it down. Vibes are the emotional signals a person gives out to those around them with their body language and social interactions. Vibrations are not verbal or audible emissions from you. They are simply what you put out into the universe. Even thoughts can give off vibrations. Are you thinking negative things about the people around you or yourself or your environment? People can sense that. They may not know exactly what you are thinking, but they just know things feel…off. The last thing you want as a host, is for your guests to feel "*off.*" Once people are turned off by the energy of a person or place, they can be reluctant to return.

In order to avoid this, we have to think about the fact that we must focus on our thoughts. If they are the components about us that give off negative feelings, then that's what we must handle first and foremost. Constantly be aware of your thoughts and how they may be impacting your interactions with others. If you are a little skeptical, or still may be having a hard time conceptualizing the idea of vibrations, I ask you to consider that we are impacted by vibrations all day.

Energies within our environment can certainly alter how we feel. Different energy sources emit frequencies and we receive them. However, if you've ever tried to tune into a radio station while driving in a remote location, you know how unclear the sound comes through. Human energy works the same way. What you experience in life largely depends on the frequency that you're tuned into and the energy that you put out into the world.

At any given moment, a person's vibration can change. This is because someone's vibe is a reflection of the thoughts and feelings that they're carrying at the moment. The next time you find yourself stuck in traffic, take a look at the people in other cars. I bet you'll be able to spot a few different types of energies; from the person who's chill and just enjoying their music, to the person that's visibly irritated and trying to find ways to cut through traffic. As you can imagine, you would feel quite different in each of these cars.

Energy is a currency. It's like a two-way system between you and everything else in the world that gives and receives vibrations. This encompasses the Golden Rule, "Do unto others as you would have them do unto you" (Matthew 7:12). Because there is this constant exchange between us and the external environment, we want to make sure we're putting out what we would like to come back. If not, then we could experience a flood of negativity that throws us off even more. Then we are stuck in this negative cycle of receiving negative energy and putting it out, just to receive even more negativity. This is the opposite of what we would like to cultivate. That's why it's important to break this cycle, if it's something you are having issues with, or to at least know about it, to avoid it altogether.

The best way to avoid this situation is to recognize your own vibe and focus your energy to give and attract blessings. First and foremost, you are your own host. What this means, is that having a deep understanding of your own energy strengthens your likelihood of guiding an entire group through a positive experience. If your own internal settings still need to calibrate, don't be afraid to look inward to see what might be calling for your attention. Focusing on energy from the inside out is the best way to attract the experiences you want out of life while being of service to others.

"The effect of raising your vibration - Once you tap into this power and learn how to shift your energetic

vibration, you'll start to notice real change. People will want to be around you. They'll feel elevated by your presence, possibly without even knowing why. You'll be more vibrant, more attractive in all ways, even smarter and sharper. You'll feel the change, too! When you're connected to your truth you feel energized, joyful, more inspired and more at ease. Raise your vibes and enjoy the results."
— Gabby Bernstein

This sentiment underscores the true power of human energy and it sheds light on why being in touch with your vibration is imperative. People gravitate towards positive energy just like they are attracted to good smells, harmonizing music, and other appealing stimulations in the world. We are able to read and pick up on these positive emissions, which are amplified simply from being around others who are emitting these same positive feelings. Think about it as "your vibe attracts your tribe." Heart-centered people want to be around others who also display a willingness to love another. Whereas people who have had painful experiences with love and affection may associate these things with trauma over time and begin to shy away from heart-centered people; whether this behavior is done consciously or outside of awareness. We all have a responsibility to preserve and protect our own energy because doing so is what ensures we can be of service to the people and spaces in the most need of a compassionate presence.

Without needing to express anything verbally, vibes are what people really hold on to. This speaks to why it's so important to be aware of your intentions while hosting and the decisions made throughout the process. If material aspects, such as decorations, preparations, or logistics, lead to overwhelming feelings, trying to elicit joy from guests may not work out as favorably as one would hope. People can pick up on stress and worry, making it difficult to be fully present in the moment and enjoy what you've put together. Worse, guests may even internalize the host's state of being overwhelmed by turning it into guilt. In other words, people can easily feel uncomfortable or unwelcomed to feel joy because they begin to realize their enjoyment comes at the host's emotional expense. Hosts are certainly allowed to feel. Again, it's all about recognizing how, when, and where that energy is expressed.

Gabby Bernstein touches on this by saying, "…to help them see how their vibes are speaking louder than their words. The reason everything keeps falling flat is that their energy isn't sustaining the experience." No matter what you say to try and convince people to have a good time, your feelings and thoughts about the event are the key to unlocking a warmhearted atmosphere.

That's why it's essential to have rationales for the steps that you take in planning gatherings and you'll want those actions to fuel you instead of draining your energy supply. Knowing yourself and how you work is extremely helpful here. For example, if preparing a large meal is just not your thing, consider ways to remove this stressor. You can even turn the alternative into a creative way to involve the group! I once attended a dinner where instead of pushing herself beyond limits, the host researched locally-owned restaurants and had guests vote on their top pick to support. Three things were accomplished here: 1) Our host anticipated her stress levels and took action to avoid burnout; 2) The event turned into a social mission to support small businesses within the community; 3) Other guests and I felt even more connected since we were given a say in the details.

If you do find yourself unable to avoid the stressors of an event that is largely based on logistics rather than the intent to connect, remaining clear on the event's purpose will help see you through. Whether you are hosting a girl's night, welcoming loved ones for the holidays, or celebrating a milestone birthday, the vibe is what creates an exceptional experience. It's the pulse that beats nonstop, which you will bring to life through your subtle touches of thoughtful hospitality. Philippians 4:8 (NIV) echo's this same sentiment:

> "Finally, brothers and sisters, whatever is true, whatever is noble, whatever is right, whatever is pure, whatever is lovely, whatever is admirable—if anything is excellent or praiseworthy—think about such things."

Energy flow is a continuous cycle that can't be destroyed or created. All you can do is transfer it from one thing/person to another. That's what your job is as the Community Cultivator. Become an expert at managing your own energy and then begin the work of impacting others simply from being around them and bringing everyone close together. Control your thoughts and feelings and watch the transformation that ensues in your personal relationships thereafter.

As the cultivator of community, you should feel empowered that you have the ability to influence the whole vibe of your event, but it can also be an intimidating responsibility. Genuity of your actions will help make this gift really feel like a gift. When you have nothing but good intentions behind your drive to bring people together, then it is a lot easier to emit good thoughts and feelings. So, remember, at the end of the day intention is something that is a benefit to you as well as to your guests.

Chapter Ten
Feel It.

Open the heart, feel the vibe…the vibe of love. This vibe feels like home to me.
— Parr Winn

With a greater understanding of vibrations, let's now expand on what it means to feel the vibe and guide the energy within your get-together. We talked about how to be aware of our own vibe, but now we are going to go beyond ourselves. Let's explore what it looks like to be aware of the energy around you and within your circle and what to do if it does feel off.

Managing the vibe is a process that begins well before planned events come to fruition. Actually, one of the first aspects to think about when inviting people in is how you want them to feel in your presence. As you're considering what type of get-together you would like to host, imagine or visualize how you'd like those within your circle to feel while you have their time and presence. Recognize the early planning stages as an opportunity to be proactive about what sort of aura you would like the event to have. To put it differently, what type of vibes do you want to serve? While determining how you want guests to feel during the time that you have them in your presence is preplanned, it's also important to be flexible and allow for the natural flux of an event. There are plenty of ways one might go about preparing for their gathering in advance, but it's impossible to foresee or control every single microscale detail. As an intentional host, your role is to provide a space that gives rise to meaningful connections. Let that focus sit at the forefront of your mind throughout the get-together. We're all humans, after all. People might arrive late. Someone might be confused about an aspect you've already explained in great detail. Whatever the case may be, remember your purpose as a community leader and let that guide you.

Throughout the event, you observe the room and find that people's spirits are not quite where you'd like them to be. Do not fear. This is an excellent sign! Why? Well for starters, congratulations for having that heightened sense of awareness. The ability to assess the energy in the room or perform a vibe check, means that actions can then be taken to influence it in the best ways. For example, a mindful host will notice if children and adult guests aren't quite vibing in a shared space. Perhaps this host prepared another room where children can safely play among themselves as their parents and other adult guests enjoy each other's company nearby. Noticing that the two age groups have separate interests and needs and then doing something to accommodate both groups can turn a chaotic space into an absolute pleasure for everyone.

Also, remember to periodically check in with yourself as well. There may be a need to identify any internal thoughts, beliefs or feelings barring you from tapping into deeper levels of intimacy. In any area of life, self-preservation is necessary. You simply cannot pour from an empty cup! Checking in with yourself first will help ensure you have enough in your cup to pour into others when they need it and are ready to receive. Further, we often underestimate our own ability to influence outcomes, especially if multiple people are involved. Yet, as a community leader, that is a large part of your role! Starting with your own mindset, what else can be done to cultivate the energy that will most benefit your guests?

An effective and discreet way to keep track of different vibes is to practice discernment, which is the ability to differentiate between what is constructive or advantageous, versus what is not. In this context, discernment is a powerful mind tool to use as you assess the energy of your gathering. As you observe, you can make informed decisions about whether or not aspects within the atmosphere are serving the group. Considering society's growing interest in self-preservation and self-care practices, we have become more keen on deciding what is fruitful as opposed to futile. Maintaining this level of awareness will help you enhance the potency of your event because you'll be ready to guide your guests beyond surface level interactions to reach profound levels of genuine intimacy.

The ability to acknowledge what's essential for connection is of interest because it's possible to run into a situation where clearing energy that distracts from your circle's mission is necessary. As an intentional host, you're not only responsible for your own vibe, but also maintaining a safe space for everyone in attendance to feel welcomed and wanted. Therefore, detaching from any aspects of the gathering that work against your vision is warranted if it means preserving the health of your circle. Bear in mind, situations like this could even call for the need to detach from individuals that may not align with the group's mission or vision, which can and should be done gracefully. Of course, we are not looking to exclude anyone or make people feel as if they aren't enough. That's the last thing we want! However, if you look closely at any community there's typically a system in place to assess one's quality of fit as it relates to everyone else. If you've ever interviewed with a company that conducts several rounds of interviews, each time with a different person, you were likely being vetted to make sure you align with where the company is headed. Or, if you've noticed many Facebook groups require new interests to answer a few questions before joining to see if there's a shared sense of community values. Now, by no means am I suggesting you hand your guests a questionnaire upon arrival or put them through a hazing process just to see if they're a good fit for a group dinner! Rather, simply be aware of the responsibility a community leader has in feeling out the energy of the group and protecting as to benefit the overall mission: to create meaningful connection.

Clearing counterproductive energy can seem unsettling, but it doesn't have to be. Applying the *Social Exchange Theory,* which again suggests people assess connections based on risks versus rewards, we will identify some parameters for you to consider whenever you are doing a vibe check. Social exchange theory simply looks at different types of social interaction and the cost/ benefit-risk relationship. Essentially, if the benefits outweigh the risks, then the interaction is likely to continue forward. However, if the risks outweigh the benefits, then the interaction will be fairly limited. Social interaction happens in societies all over the world and can help to stabilize society or cause change in a society or community. But all social interactions don't happen for the same reason. According to this theory, there are actually five different types of common interaction: exchange, competition, conflict, cooperation and accommodation. The details of each are beyond the scope of this book. However, the main takeaway is that there are some interactions that are going to be mutually beneficial, while others are going to be a lopsided relationship. In biblical hospitality, we want to see equality. Everyone equally benefitting from interactions in a tribe. When this turns out to not be the case and someone takes more than they give, then that can throw off the whole equilibrium of the event.

If something feels uneasy about the atmosphere of your event, shift your focus to the human aspects. Superficial vibes aren't something that we can afford to be misled by because it threatens the stability of the social circle we are trying to build. Therefore, it's important to exude what you'd like to attract while also having the grace to consider why someone may be giving surface level interaction. Their behavior could reveal a lack of comfort or trust, lack of acceptance or timidness. It's up to you to figure out the difference between ill-intentions and innocent reservation.

Here is where emotional intelligence plays a huge role while hosting. Emotional intelligence is the ability to understand and manage your own emotions and those of the people around you. People with a high degree of emotional intelligence know what they're feeling, what their emotions mean, and how these emotions can affect other people. As the host, or community developer, there is a great advantage being able to understand and manage your own emotions and the group's.

When we can tap into how others are feeling, as well as how we are feeling, we can better manage our events. We know what it's missing and what we can do to possibly fix it. Before jumping into action though, to fix the vibe and potentially be "extra," there are some steps to take so the changes don't have the opposite intended affect. This is what it means to be socially aware, or have social awareness. As a host, it's rather important to continuously develop the skill of social awareness because it will strengthen your ability to pick up on a vibe shift and know how to return it to your original goals. Social awareness is the ability to know what's going on, socially, around you and how to manage your feelings as well as your guests. For example, if someone says something that makes others feel uncomfortable, are you able to pick up on this? Even if you didn't find that it made you uncomfortable? This is part of your responsibility of creating environments where everyone feels safe.

Once an air of malaise is sensed, hit the pause button for a moment. Before slipping into feelings of discouragement or flooding guests with questions about their wellbeing, let's take a step back to see what is really off. It's better to be direct and intentional when tweaking the vibe, than very broad and trying to fire hose everything, hoping it makes it better. It's a waste of energy and may not even solve the problem. After taking the pause, the next step is to explore the why. This is when we step out of our own shoes and think about how someone else may be feeling about what's happening. This perspective-taking helps us make adjustments that directly address our guests' needs. Finally, after shifting the vibe, the next important part is to learn from what happened and carry it into subsequent events. Each time you do a vibe check, there is something to learn about influencing the energy within a space. This way you'll be equipped with experience that helps you remain agile as the host of future gatherings.

The final thing to really consider when going about changing a vibe is your intention behind the shift. Remember, we have to be very aware of what our intentions are as to make sure they are pure, loving, and in support of our community. Think about the future implications of your current actions and the broader meaning.

As an example of what this looks like in practice, I'll reference a practice of an African tribe that resonates. In this particular tribe, when a member does something wrong, instead of shaming the individual they take them to the center of their village. The community surrounds them for two days and everyone speaks of all the good things the person in the center has done. This community believes all people are inherently good and worthy of love. Yet, we make mistakes. This practice reminds those who may temporarily steer off track from community values that they are unconditionally loved and supported, which can certainly encourage acts of goodwill moving forward.

Chapter Eleven

Create It.

Don't adapt to the energy of the room. Influence the energy in the room.

It's finally here! The evening you and your girls or your guys have been planning to connect, and simply enjoy each other's company. You are the host and you are ready! The weather is perfect, energy is high, and conversation is flowing freely; but will your efforts in creating the perfect vibe successfully satisfy your guests throughout the event? Here you will learn more about creating, facilitating, and appreciating an intentional vibe- all essential aspects of being a stunning host and offering a truly unforgettable gathering.

When hosting, the vibe is undeniably the most important element of your gathering. It is the invisible, yet ever-present energy that circulates throughout your environment. The vibe that you create is what leaves a lasting impression on your guests. It's what people will remember, talk about and maybe even attempt to recreate for their own events! That's because the ambiance speaks to quality and your guests deserve nothing short of that. As the host, it is up to you to establish the character or atmosphere of your environment- a desirable one at that!

Just so it's easier to keep this in mind, now that you have made it to the end of this conversation, I want to promote you from Community Cultivator to *Vibe Creator*. With this new title in mind, you are constantly reminded that the important part about hosting others is to maintain a vibe that uplifts and makes your guests feel welcome. As the vibe creator, it is important to know that your biggest priority is the strategy of how you are going to create the vibe and the impact that you hope your event has on your guests. When we talk about strategy, I'm not necessarily talking about the logistics (place, food, décor, etc.), I am talking about how you are going to go about creating this vibe. What are you going to have your guests do or how are you going to get them to talk? What kind of people are you going to bring together? These are some factors to consider when thinking about creating a vibe.

Impact is also something to remain mindful of. What is the desired effect of your event? How do you want people to feel as they are leaving and during the span of time prior to your next event? When planning these are things to consider because then they fall into your strategy. If you know how you would like to impact your community, then that will make it easier to come up with an effective strategy to accomplish this impact. Being thoughtful and deliberate in how you design every major aspect of your event also contributes to the impact. You don't just put things together just because; but you have a legitimate reason and expected outcome of your decision. This may help with your thoughts and feelings so you are emitting positive energy still. Everything was so intentional that you are actually excited to implement those things, instead of potentially too stressed out to enjoy your own event.

While planning, also remember to stay flexible. Like we talked about in the last chapter, things happen and you will not always be in 100% control of what is happening. That's okay and something you should expect that going in. In accepting that, you can choose to remain agile as life plays out the way it will. Don't get burdened with logistics and allow individuals to have their flexibility in choice about certain aspects of your event. But also provide a solid framework for guests to work within. This way you are providing a relaxed environment that has some form of organization. It's a win-win situation.

One of the last things I'm going to mention about your new role as a vibe creator is don't forget to empower others and delegate work. Know what you are good at and stay in that lane. But if someone else is better at something than you are and has the time to dedicate to your event, then let them do it. You'll not only take some stress off your plate, but also increase the diversity of input of the event. This adds to the value of your vibe, as some of your guests who had some input will respect it since they contributed.

To simplify this further, you'll be sure to please by implementing these key essentials to creating a vibe:

> **Know your audience:** Select activities or stations that will be engaging, but not overwhelming to guests. Knowing your audience is all about being mindful of both introverted and extroverted guests. Your extroverted guests will be ready and willing to jump right into networking, competitive icebreakers, or any other high-contact activities. Just what your event needs to thrive! Meanwhile,

introverted guests are often less pronounced and likely to be more interested. As a host one should be mindful that they are not to be overlooked. Sufficient pre-planning will prepare you to satisfy a variety of interests and comfort levels.

Involve your guests: Give guests tasks to help you facilitate the event and provoke conversation. Guests tend to participate more when facilitation is a shared experience. Incorporating interactive entertainment is an effective way to get your guest talking, keep the group engaged, and share some of the responsibility in maintaining the character of your event. When energy is high, the vibe is infectious!

Ambiance is necessary: The more senses you appeal to, the better! In addition to music, captivate your guests by providing a visual experience as well. Create ambiance with great music that suits the vibe you are trying to cultivate. If your event calls for music, remember to be mindful of volume when conversation is involved. A small adjustment in volume could prevent your guests from the need to yell and rather allow them to engage comfortably.

You really want to create an experience that is so emotionally stimulating that it will stick with individuals far beyond their attendance at your event. This is when you know that you were successful in creating the vibe that you wanted. Your goals can be different for different events, but at the end of the day, you may want to have this common feeling of inclusion and participation being a consistent measure of success.

Your event is simply a culmination of smaller events or moments. So, as your event is progressing along, have your guests do something impactful. They can share things with the group or you all can participate in some sort of impactful community activity. Depending on your group, perhaps you can have specific activities geared towards their growth in different aspects of life. Maybe introverts could practice writing and saying affirmations. Find ways that people can be authentically themselves and you will create successful memories that will leave your guests wanting more interactions like that one. Your event doesn't have to be emotionally taxing or heavy, but it should be intentional. Remember, intentional hosting is the basis for everything we have talked about throughout this entire book. If you don't have intentions, then you don't really have a solid base to keep your event headed in the direction you would like it to. Remember, at the end of the day, just getting together produces this sort of magic as we tap into each other's pain, pleasure, excitement, and joy. Try not to mistake the magic coming from logistics alone.

When you invite people into your presence, understand that everyone has something going on in their life. True hospitality is acknowledging that and for the sake of a couple of hours, provide an escape with the intention of curating an experience that renews their spirit. In order to create the best environment to achieve that, consider the following questions:

- What is the reason I am hosting this gathering?
- What may most of my guests need from me to leave feeling fulfilled?

- How can I create an atmosphere where everyone can be themselves?
- What are some ways in which I introduce love and support into the places of my guests that are broken?

Maybe the next time you ask a friend to go to dinner, you go with the intention to sit with them and listen because they have felt so overrun and unheard by others. Perhaps you invite your dear friends over and have a question hat that generates deep discussions about what everyone is doing to keep their faith while dealing with such a hard time or navigating the different stages of life. These are all examples of intentional hosting and there is a greater focus on impact rather than the logistics. After enjoying some good times with loved ones and friends, talking about what may be going on in everyone's lives and incorporating Jesus where He may have been left out, everyone has a better chance of feeling renewed and you get to feel satisfied. Even though everyone still has to go back to their own lives, they may be going back with a different perspective or rejuvenated spirit.

How can I create an atmosphere where everyone can be themselves? When considering the atmosphere, your first thought may be how to make it perfect, how to ensure everyone will have a good time. As you are hosting, if you are anything like me, you walk around and read the room. Are people smiling, dancing (if there's music), chatting with one another. Or do people appear disengaged, or even upset? Either way, you are completely caught up in building the vibe, then either maintaining it or fixing it. But all of that takes away from your ability to genuinely build community with one another.

Here is something else to keep in mind when talking about atmosphere. If your atmosphere is not real, then how can you expect your guests to feel comfortable enough to be their real selves. You know that as soon as you walk in somewhere that seems so put together and high class, you immediately feel the need to change up your tune so you fit in. But the whole time, you're just worried that someone will catch you and call you out for not belonging. How can you focus on your spirit and fellowshipping with those around you when you're just trying to keep your mask on? You can't. And you don't want your guests to be experiencing this mental conundrum in your presence. You don't want them to resent you asking them to come because it was more of a hassle than a blessing. You don't want them trying to impress you and you trying to impress them. It's a circus on both sides. So, when thinking about your environment, really think about authenticity. Who are you, not who you want people to *think* you are. Real versus phony vibes are really easy to spot out.

As you are considering hosting people, just remember to tap into who you really are. This takes away the distractions of performing a show for people. It's easy to be yourself. It's hard to be someone else. When you are presenting your home or your life for the mess that it truly is (trust me, we all have messy lives. So, don't feel any type of way about this), then you invite others to be just as vulnerable. Vulnerability is an essential state for biblical hosting. It allows people to tear down their walls so there can be true enlightenment and encouragement. Everyone is open to sharing their fears, insecurities, and doubts because they trust you and the environment enough to do so. Once all of that is out on the table, then you can begin having a deep spiritual movement to encourage and exhort one another. Authenticity and vulnerability are the two words to keep in mind when considering your atmosphere.

Chapter Twelve

The Vibe Creator's Workbook

We've reached the conclusion of our journey through intentional hosting. Give yourself a pat on the back because you've digested quite a bit of information about an extremely layered topic. While there are multiple layers to hosting, I hope that breaking it down as such has made the concept of inviting others into your space feel more approachable and purposeful.

Our collective wellbeing depends on heart-centered individuals like you and I to go into communities and create the types of experiences that deepen our commitment to one another. We will have nothing if we do not learn how to cherish each other, and intentional hosting is the key to bridging any gaps we may currently have.

Remember, hosting is what you make it. A virtual connection is just as much of an opportunity to honor someone as an in-person visit, perhaps just a different approach and mindset. Know that what our world is experiencing is temporary and we will one day arrive at a sense of normalcy…our new normal. When we do, let's commit to showing up for one another in ways that edify. Let's exercise awareness, first within ourselves, and then extend that focus outward to help enrich the lives of those around us. Lastly, let us never underestimate the power of a meaningful connection that is rooted in pure love and acceptance!

Throughout this book several chapters include thought-provoking questions to apply the material and keep your thoughts flowing. As you continue developing in your role as a community leader or intentional host, return to these questions as a way to keep yourself moving upward and onward.

The Crisis – Assessing the Damage:

1. Often, when we are separated from community (family, friends, coworkers) for an extended period of time our well-being becomes compromised. How has the global pandemic affected you and your relationship to community?

2. In what ways were you/have you been able to connect with your community through this crisis?

3. We've learned that in order to show up for our communit(ies), we have to be able to show up for ourselves, as well. How have you been intentional about connecting with your true self?

    a. Let's do a quick vibe check - Are you pouring from an empty cup?

Community is at the Heart of the Solution:

4. *Recognizing our communities* – Take a moment to take an inventory of the communities you are connected to. Identify key people in those communities and make an assessment on whether or not this group of people could use a little more attention and effort from you:

Type of Community:	Community Members:	Community of Focus:
Use the descriptions in Chapter 3 to identify the type of community.	List the names of people that make up this group.	Determine if this community should be an area of focus for you.

5. Energy can be contagious. In what ways can hosting elevate the vibe within your community?

6. As a host, how can you help people feel as comfortable with who they are as possible?

The Mindset Shift:

7. In an earlier chapter, I ask *"What is hosting doing to you physically, mentally and spiritually?"* Take a few moments to think about this honestly, jot down a few thoughts.

8. List what are the most overwhelming aspects of hosting for you. The answer is different for each individual.

   1.

   2.

   3.

   4.

   5.

9. Once you've made your list, let's begin to brainstorm why this may be and how you can overcome it. Complete the statement for each.

_____overwhelms me, because

```
┌─────────────────────────────────────────────┐
│                                               │
│                                               │
│                                               │
└─────────────────────────────────────────────┘
```

_____overwhelms me, because

```
┌─────────────────────────────────────────────┐
│                                               │
│                                               │
│                                               │
└─────────────────────────────────────────────┘
```

_____overwhelms me, because

```
┌─────────────────────────────────────────────┐
│                                               │
│                                               │
│                                               │
└─────────────────────────────────────────────┘
```

_____overwhelms me, because

```
┌─────────────────────────────────────────────┐
│                                               │
│                                               │
│                                               │
└─────────────────────────────────────────────┘
```

10. Take an inventory of those items that overwhelm. Think about what potential solution could help alleviate what overwhelms you so you can focus on the most impactful aspects of your event:

11. Outsource/Hire

12. Ask a friend or a guest to assist

13. Eliminate

Four-Point Vibe Check:

Primary Focus:

Invite your guests to the center of your event. What may most of my guests need from me to leave feeling fulfilled?

Purpose of Gathering:

Plan with the end in mind - With intentional hosting, it is important to think about how you want people to leave your presence feeling. The goal is to uplift, connect, remind community that they are supported. What is the primary reason I am hosting this gathering?

Intimacy:

Within intimate relationships, people make time to learn new things and collect new experiences together. What tools can you use to facilitate trust building and intimacy at your next gathering?

Inclusive environment:

Gathering in a space where your importance and value are validated by others feels noticeably different than occupying a space where you are overlooked and disregarded, right? Offer your guests the gift of hospitality by mindfully cultivating an environment where people aren't left wondering where they stand in relation to others. How can I create an atmosphere where everyone can be themselves?

Notes

Agrawal, Radha. Belong: *Find Your People, Create Community, and Live a More Connected Life*. Illustrated, Workman Publishing Company, 2018.

Andreatta, Britt. "Beyond Diversity: The Science of Inclusion and Belonging." *Training Industry,* 12 Mar. 2020, trainingindustry.com/articles/diversity-equity-and-inclusion/beyond-diversity-the-science-of-inclusion-and-belonging/#:%7E:text=We%20all%20know%20that%20diversity,Innovation%20and%20creative%20problem%2Dsolving.

Bahr, Howard M., et al. "Loneliness: A Sourcebook of Current Theory, Research and Therapy." *Contemporary Sociology,* vol. 13, no. 2, 1984, p. 203. *Crossref*, doi:10.2307/2068915.

Bernstein, Gabrielle Bernstein. "*Vibes Speak Louder than Words.*" *Gabby Bernstein*, 25 Aug. 2020, gabbybernstein.com/vibes-speak-louder-than-words.

Cacioppo, John, and William Patrick. *Loneliness: Human Nature and the Need for Social Connection*. Reprint, W. W. Norton & Company, 2009.

Church, Crossbridge. "Hospitality Is Stewardship." *Crossbridge Church,* 25 Sept. 2014, crossbridgemiami.squarespace.com/pastor-felipes-blog/blog/2014/9/25/hospitality-is-stewardship.

Heinrich, Liesl M., and Eleonora Gullone. "The Clinical Significance of Loneliness: A Literature Review." *Clinical Psychology Review,* vol. 26, no. 6, 2006, pp. 695–718. *Crossref,* doi:10.1016/j.cpr.2006.04.002.

Holyfireorg. "WHAT DOES IT MEAN TO NOT FORSAKE THE ASSEMBLING OF OURSELVES?" *The Flaming Herald,* 12 June 2017, theflamingherald.wordpress.com/2017/06/12/what-does-it-mean-to-not-forsake-the-assembling-of-ourselves.

Millington, Richard. "Different Types Of Communities." *FeverBee*, 6 Sept. 2016, www.feverbee.com/different-types-of-communities.

Nelson, Shasta. *Frientimacy: How to Deepen Friendships for Lifelong Health and Happiness*. Illustrated, Seal Press, 2016.

Preston, Cheryl. "The True Meaning of Forsake Not Assembling Together." *LetterPile - Writing and Literature*, 2 Apr. 2020, letterpile.com/religion/The-True-Meaning-of-Forsake-Not-Assembling-Together.

"The Power of Biblical Hospitality." *The Exchange | A Blog by Ed Stetzer*, www.christianitytoday.com/edstetzer/2019/august/power-of-biblical-hospitality-entertainment-jesus.html. Accessed 16 Nov. 2020.

Vogl, Charles. *The Art of Community: Seven Principles for Belonging*. 1st ed., Berrett-Koehler Publishers, 2016.

Wilkie, Jack. "Misunderstanding 'Forsaking the Assembly.'" *Focus Press*, 18 Mar. 2020, www.focuspress.org/2020/03/17/misunderstanding-forsaking-the-assembly.

Zevallos, Zuleyka. "Sociology of Community." *The Other Sociologist*, 23 Apr. 2019, othersociologist.com/2013/11/20/sociology-of-community.

Alexis Hudson Moore
Hosted by the Moore Collective
Website: hostedbytmc.com
Email: Hello@hostedbytmc.com

Additional resources and copies of
When We All Get Together:
A Guide for the Intentional Host
are available on
hostedbytmc.com
Amazon
or order at your local bookstore

CPSIA information can be obtained
at www.ICGtesting.com
Printed in the USA
LVHW010414070121
675505LV00003B/325